EY UP MI DUCK!

Dialect of Derbyshire and the East Midlands

RICHARD SCOLLINS & JOHN TITFORD

COUNTRYSIDE BOOKS
NEWBURY BERKSHIRE

COUNTRYSIDE BOOKS
3 Catherine Road
Newbury, Berkshire

To view our complete range of books,
please visit us at
www.countrysidebooks.co.uk

ISBN 1 85306 658 3

Produced through MRM Associates Ltd., Reading
Printed by Woolnough Bookbinding Ltd., Irthlingborough

CONTENTS

ACKNOWLEDGEMENTS

A list of acknowledgements could run to pages, but we would like to extend a special word of thanks to the following helpers and contributors, without whom this work could never have made its appearance:

Brian Aldred
David Amedra
Frank Aram
Mr and Mrs Ash
Ian Baird
Peter Baker
Barry
John Barsby, John Hobson, BBC Radio Nottingham
Jim Beardsley, Sr. & Jr.
John F. Beardsley
Jim & Jackie Beighton
Walter Beighton
Tyna Belfield
Nelson Bestwick
Ken Bettle
Joan Blant
Mrs Boddy
Anne Brown & Dianne
Pete Brown
Bill Butler
Frank Camm
Jean Cashford
Doreen Chapman
Danny Corns
Mrs J. Derbyshire
Harriet Ellis
Wilf Evans
Jack Fearn
Dennis Featherstone
Richard Field
Ray Fletcher, M.P.
Roy, Pearl, Michael & Heather Flockton

Jack Fowkes
Lionel Fryer
Stephen Full
Robert Gathercole
Harvey Good
Alfred Harris
Dorothy & Jack Hartley
Dorothy & Bert Heale
Jack & Edie Hill
Jim Hollingworth
Miss Maud Hollingworth
D. G. Holroyd, Esq.
Roland Horridge
Brenda Hunt
Ray Huthwaite & family
Ilkeston & District Local History Society
The pupils, staff, & canteen staff of Ilkeston School
The staff of Ilkeston Library
Rev. J. M. Innes
The late Mr Ernie Jephecote
Mary Johnson
Alf Keightley
Martin Kirk
Graham Knight, John Derby, Dave Newman, Radio Trent
Jack Lally
Sidney T. Lee
Lou
Andrew Manley

Diane Martin
Bruce Miles, Midlands Today BBC TV
Roger Mitchell
Keith Moon
Angela Osborn
Howard Peach
Trevor Pear
Mel Pearce
Peter Pheasant
David Popple
Alison Raju
Phil Rowley
Mrs O. G. Scollins
Simon Shaw, BBC Radio Derby
K. L. Smith, Esq.
J. Barrie Smith, Esq.
David Sommerlad
Peter Stevenson
Sam Taylor
Helen Thompson
Mr & Mrs S. H. Titford
Willie Tucker
Alan Tudor
Jack Tudor
Owen Watson
Charley Webster
Mr & Mrs H. Whitehead
Jim Winfield
John & Sue Winfield
Harold Wood
Cyril Woodcock
Ian Wordsworth
Brian & Derek Wright

FOREWORD

SUPWIYO? . . . DUNNA WITTLE . . . EH COULDNA STOP A PIG IN AN ENTRY . . . IT'S GERRIN A BIT BLACK OWER BILL'S MOTHA'S . . . EH'S THRAY SHAITS TE T'WIND . . . LET'S AY A GLEG . . . PURREMINEER . . . WORREEWEEISSEN? . . . AH'M GOOIN TER TON ME BIKE RAIRND . . . OWD YER SWEAT . . . GERRIMOFFOM . . . 'IS EYES STOOD AAHT LIKE CHAPEL 'AT PEGS . . . WELL, AH'LL GOO T'AAR AASE!

Can people in the East Midlands really be speaking the English language? When East Midlanders travel to far-away places elsewhere in the British Isles, should they be taking an interpreter with them?

It's one of the glories of life in Britain that even in the 21st century there is a rich diversity of dialect and accent being used on an everyday basis by people who have long rejected the efforts of educators and others to tell them that they are deviating from an established standard and should fall into line immediately.

Television and radio have brought several previously unfamiliar dialects and accents to the attention of listeners and viewers all over the country. Broad Glaswegian or Geordie speakers do not sound so strange any more to a generation brought up on Billy Connolly and on television programmes like *Byker Grove*.

Right in the heart of England, however, there is a form of speech which is common to much of Derbyshire, Nottinghamshire, Leicestershire and Staffordshire which has never had the media 'treatment' and still surprises the unwary. It's far from being broad Yorkshire, and it has little enough in common with the speech of Birmingham and the Black Country. Not all East Midland speakers sound the same, but the *Ey Up Mi Duck!* books, in setting out to celebrate the speech of Derbyshire, struck a chord with people over a much wider area.

The *Ey Up Mi Duck!* books came about as a result of a chance meeting in a pub in Stanton by Dale, near Ilkeston in Derbyshire, between Richard Scollins, a locally-born writer and internationally-known artist, and John Titford, a Londoner who was working as a teacher in Ilkeston. The subsequent friendship and professional collaboration between Richard and John resulted in the publication of three *Ey Up Mi Duck!* books and a long-playing record of the same name. Finding no publisher who would take on a book on dialect which was both serious and yet funny at the same time, the two authors set about publishing *Ey Up Mi Duck!* themselves in December 1976. Sales soon reached tens of thousands; people

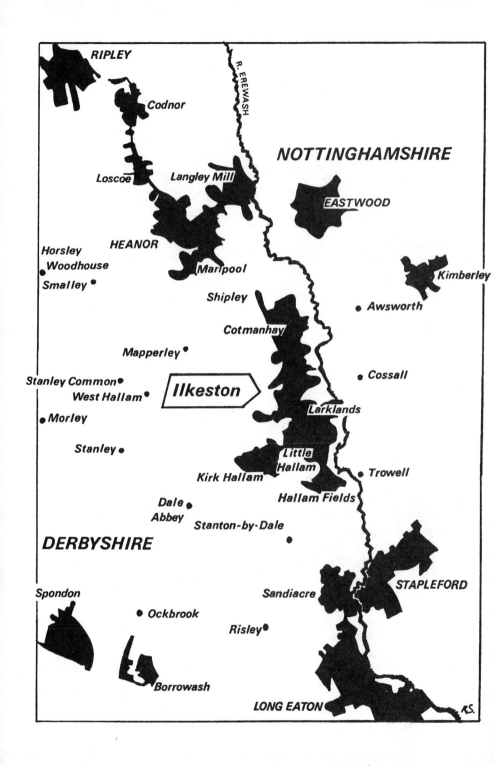

bought copies of the book for themselves, gave them away as presents, handed them to visitors from abroad, or sent them to friends and relatives in far-flung lands to remind them of home.

Tragically, in 1992, Richard Scollins collapsed at his house in Kirk Hallam and died at the age of 45. His memory has been kept alive since by exhibitions of his art work, by the establishment of a nature area at Ilkeston School and by fund-raising folk music and dance events, the proceeds of which have allowed the Richard Scollins fund to make cash awards to many people of all ages working in the arts locally. Much of the writing and the illustrations in *Ey Up Mi Duck!* itself, meanwhile, bear eloquent testimony to the talents of this remarkable man.

Still the demand for copies of *Ey Up Mi Duck!* has grown, as a new generation of young people has been intrigued to read a book which celebrates their way of speech. At last *Ey Up Mi Duck!* has again been re-published — this time with the essence of all three parts included in one volume, and with the addition of extra material from Richard Scollins' *Almost Totally Insane Derbyshire Look at British History in Pictures*, published in 1978.

WELL, AH'LL GOO T'AAR AASE!

John Titford
September 2000

Introduction

While we hope you will find this book both amusing and entertaining, the underlying reason for its existence is, in fact, a serious one. The basis for our little saga about Ilkeston is an attempt to put into print something of the fast-disappearing dialect of this area — 'Erewash Valley speech', we may term it. The book does not pretend to be either an exhaustive study of a dialect or a detailed local history — there are far too many gaps for that — but we do hope that it captures some of the warmth and humour to be found among the stolid inhabitants of this most underrated corner of Derbyshire. This project reflects something of the character of the people we've interviewed — a different set of informants would have resulted in a somewhat different offering, but what we do wish to stress is that everything you'll find in these pages is deeply rooted in reality — even the 'pub conversations' are taken from tape recordings we made.

Our main concern has been with the everyday speech of Ilkeston (more traditionally referred to as 'Ilson') and district, and we make no apologies for concentrating mainly on the full traditional dialect of the area, rather than on the watered-down version of it which most Ilkestonians now speak. In fact, although this extreme form of the dialect is on its way out, vigorous pockets of resistance remain, and not all the strongest dialect speakers are elderly people, either.

Since we will in the course of this book use both the words 'dialect' and 'accent' frequently, and since these two terms may seem to be somewhat loosely applied at times (it is always difficult to be very precise when talking about language) we ought at this stage to define the difference between them. In simple terms, accent is a matter of pronunciation, whereas dialect involves vocabulary, special phrases, and even a different grammar. When we speak of a person's accent, we usually mean that he is speaking what is known as 'Standard English', but with distinctive features of pronunciation. Stanley Ellis, an expert in dialect from Leeds University, puts it like this:

'Dialect is a traditionally-developed correct way of speaking from the area in which it is used; accent is an attempt at speaking the standard language and modifying it in the local sort of manner'.

Let's take just one example from Ilkeston: the word 'she'. The true dialect version of this would be 'oh', whereas Standard English with a strong Ilkeston accent would give you 'shey'.

It's worth remembering that everyone has his or her own special way of speaking — we all talk a kind of personal dialect. Sometimes families have small dialect patterns of their own, some words or phrases which carry special meaning for those who are 'in the know'; and the same is true of all sorts of social groups, from Rugby Clubs to Women's Institutes. At the same time, we tend to be inconsistent in the way we use language; within the space of a couple of sentences a speaker may well pronounce the same word in two or three different ways. It's common knowledge, too, that the way we speak often varies according to the company we're in.

When we refer to 'Ilkeston dialect' we are not implying that this is a unique form of speech differing greatly from the surrounding area — merely that this is how English was and is spoken in Ilkeston. The days when one small village spoke a markedly different dialect from its neighbours are virtually gone. Thirty or forty years ago, not only would the speech of an average Ilkestonian have been unintelligible to an outsider, but it would have differed considerably from that of an inhabitant of, say, Heanor or Eastwood.[1] Nowadays, it's true that marked variations in speech over a relatively small area still sometimes occur—Derby and Nottingham accents differ considerably from 'Erewash Valley', for instance, and even within Ilkeston itself, Cotmanhay retains its reputation for very broad speech.[2] In general, however, as a result of population movements and the influence of the mass media, these differences are becoming blurred. Dialects don't change as soon as they hit a county border (they never have done; unless the border happened to be a large natural feature, such as a wide river), and except for a few surviving words and phrases, the speech on the Nottinghamshire side of this part of the Erewash Valley is more or less the same as it is on the Ilkeston side.

The criterion we've used for determining whether or not a word or phrase is 'Ilkeston' has been simply to compare it with modern 'Standard English', not with other regional dialects. For this reason a good deal of what we've included as Ilkeston dialect applies also to a much wider area — not only the rest of Derbyshire, but to most of the English North and Midlands, and even Scottish Lowlands as well — but this doesn't make it any the less 'Ilkeston'.

Modern regional dialects in England still stem basically from the different speech patterns of Old English, the Germanic language spoken by the Angles, Saxons, Jutes, and other smaller tribes who migrated to Britain during the fifth and sixth centuries

1. Mr Owen V. Watson, who describes his own dialect as the 'Tag Hill' variety, tells us that when he worked at Shipley, with people from every town and village within a four-mile radius, he always reckoned he could tell to a mile where his mates lived by the variations in their speech.

2. Cotmanhay was once more clearly separated from Ilkeston than it is now; Kelly's Directory of 1855 calls it: 'A hamlet and scattered village 1½ miles North West from Ilkeston'. In the nineteenth century its inhabitants were mainly colliers and framework knitters; even into this century, a large proportion of the miners in the Ilkeston area lived there, and children at school in the town were frequently mocked by Ilkeston pupils — many of whose parents were factory workers, and considered themselves superior to the mining fraternity — on account of their broad and distinctive Cotmanhay accents.

A.D., and who collectively referred to themselves as 'Engle' or 'Englisc'. During the eighth and ninth centuries, large settlements of Danish and Norwegian Vikings occurred, and for a time, in fact, most of England north of a line from London to Chester was under the control of the Vikings, and was known as 'The Danelaw'.

The heaviest concentration of Scandinavian settlers was in Northumbria (especially North-West England and Yorkshire); North and East Mercia (especially Derbyshire, Nottinghamshire, Leicestershire and Lincolnshire); and East Anglia. The language spoken by these people was Old Norse, a close relative of Old English, and as the two peoples gradually became intermixed, the language of the invaded absorbed that of the invaders. By this process, however, many words and phrases of Scandinavian origin passed into English, especially in the Danelaw. Even today there is a marked contrast, for instance, between the dialect spoken in North Staffordshire, which was part of the Danelaw, and that spoken in the southern end of the county, which remained in English hands. Not only does North Staffordshire speech contain many more Scandinavian words, but its use of certain vowel sounds is very similar to that found in Derbyshire, Nottinghamshire and Leicestershire-all areas of strong Danish influence. With the Norman conquest of 1066, French and Latin became the languages of Church, Court and ruling élite, and English was driven underground. By the time of the re-emergence of English as the state language in the fourteenth century, it had undergone profound changes, including the addition of a good many words of French and Latin origin. It was during this period, around 1400, that a 'standard' form of English began to appear, at a time when regional dialects were so different as to make people from the North and South of England almost totally incomprehensible to each other. Originally a South-East Midland dialect, 'Standard English' was adopted as the speech of the Court based on London, and consequently grew in status and prestige over other dialects. Because of this it was polished and refined more than other forms of English, and changed much faster. This is why regional dialects often retain older words and pronunciations which Standard English has dropped.

The higher social status of Standard English inevitably led to a movement to 'correct' the speech of other areas. The standardization of spelling[3] strengthened this movement, and by the eighteenth century, Dr Johnson was writing that 'the best general rule is to consider those as the most elegant speakers who deviate least from the written word'. This marriage between a standard written and spoken English, the growth of the public schools in the nine-

3. This standardization took place around 1700. It was largely based, however, upon the pronunciation of English prevalent in late Mediaeval times; consequently, although the new standardized spelling attempted to reflect the spoken word closely, it left us with a legacy of apparent incongruities, such as the 'k' in the word 'knight', which had once been pronounced as a separate sound . . . the word would originally have been pronounced ·something like 'kernickt'.

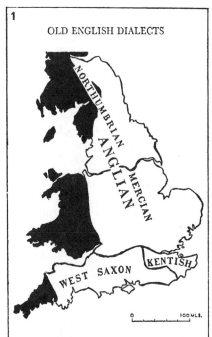

1

OLD ENGLISH DIALECTS

NORTHUMBRIAN

ANGLIAN

MERCIAN

KENTISH

WEST SAXON

0   100 MLS.

2

MIDDLE ENGLISH DIALECTS

NORTHERN

WEST MIDLAND

EAST MIDLAND

SOUTH-WESTERN

SOUTH-EASTERN

0   100 MLS.

3

ENGLISH DIALECTS IN 1887

MIDLAND

NORTHERN

MIDLAND

EASTERN

WESTERN

SOUTHERN

0   100 MLS.

Map 1. The four main dialect areas of Old English: West Saxon, Kentish, Mercian and Northumbrian (the last two of these often being grouped together as Anglian). There were certainly other dialects in this period, of which we have no record. Most surviving Old English manuscripts are in the West Saxon dialect — many of the earlier written documents were destroyed during the Viking conquests of the North and Midlands, and it was the kings of Wessex who eventually unified 'Engle-land'. Although this led to the recognition of West Saxon as a literary standard during the late Anglo-Saxon period, it is not the direct ancestor of modern Standard English, which is mainly derived from an Anglian dialect.

Map 2. English dialect areas of the mediaeval period. Note how most of Derbyshire lies in the West Midland dialect area, whilst the rest of the county (including, of course, the Erewash Valley) comes under the East Midland sector. Up until the end of the fourteenth century, authors would write English in their own regional dialects; from the fifteenth century onwards, one dialect — roughly that of the Southern part of the East Midlands — became a 'Standard English'. The South-Eastern part of England contained the capital city, and also the only two Universities, Oxford and Cambridge, within its bounds; it eventually added linguistic dominance to its social and economic pre-eminence. Standard English, originating as it did from the old Mercian region, became, in a way, a useful North-South compromise.

Map 3. English dialects based on a survey carried out towards the end of the nineteenth century. As may be observed on Map 2, it is interesting to note how far North the northern boundary of the Midland dialect area is placed. In other words, the speech of most of Lancashire and a large part of West Yorkshire is here classed as 'North Midland'.

teenth century, and the arrival of national broadcasting[4] in this century, have all combined to create a situation where correct, traditional pronunciation, grammar and vocabulary are condemned as sloppy, lazy speech. The truth is, that whilst a standard form of English is useful as a kind of dictionary to which we can refer, or use as a point of comparison, and whilst it obviously makes communication between different parts of the English-speaking world much easier, there is no question of it being more 'correct' than other forms of English. No way of speaking is intrinsically right or wrong, despite all the misguided attempts of generations of teachers and preachers to exterminate all localized forms of speech, and frequent exhortations to children to 'scrape their tongues'.[5]

Another reason why regional dialects are on the decline is that a good many of the words and phrases in traditional speech described activities that are dying out — much of the language associated with wash-day or out-moded agricultural or industrial practices, for instance, is fast disappearing. However, there is new material cropping up all the time, usually making its appearance as slang, much of which is local, despite the large body of national phrases we pick up from TV or Radio (and remember that Standard English has its own colloquial variants, its own slang). Slang is the most immediate form of dialect, what G. K. Chesterton called 'The one stream of poetry which is constantly flowing'. Some purists would hardly consider it dialect at all, but it would be ridiculous to think of 'apples and pears' (Cockney rhyming slang for 'stairs') as dialect, just because it has been in use for years, whilst ignoring a much more modern addition like 'Alan Whickers' ('knickers').

Professor Harold Orton, one of the major pioneers of dialect study in England this century, once said rather cynically: 'There are sentimentalists who are anxious that dialects should be preserved . . . but for other people to talk . . . not for themselves'.

Certainly no one wants local dialects to become museum pieces or oddities that only 'other people' use — but the more dialect is spoken, the less chance there is of that happening. What should be preserved is choice; people ought to be able to choose the way they wish to speak — language use should never be prescriptive. It's all summed up by the old fellow from Cotmanhay; asked by his son whether he should pronounce the word 'either' as 'eether' or 'eyether' he replied:

'Ayther'll dow, yothe!'

Before dealing with the regular features of Ilkeston dialect in some detail, there are three important points we'd like to make.

---

4. The Americans have their own Standard English, especially influential in the field of broadcasting, known, appropriately, as 'Network Standard English'. There is also a Standard Scottish English.

5. Attempts by educators to eradicate dialect speech have continued almost unabated, often despite official advice to the contrary: 'Teachers should not consider themselves in any sense called upon to extirpate a genuine local dialect'. (Teachers' Handbook, 1929, page 74).

In the first place, Erewash Valley speech is not particularly well known outside the district in which it is used. It seems, moreover, to have been largely ignored by scholars, and, indeed, this whole area was completely overlooked during the large-scale survey of English dialects carried out by Leeds University during the 1950s.

Secondly, it is a deceptively difficult dialect for outsiders to imitate. Those of you with an Ilkeston accent may be acquainted with people from the South who've known you for years, but who will, if called upon to imitate your speech, produce a 'Coronation Street' sort of voice. The fact is that an Erewash Valley dialect does not conform to the stock TV 'Northern' accent, and this is probably why we have yet to see an adaptation of one of D. H. Lawrence's stories which doesn't sound as if it was set in Yorkshire! Lastly, another important feature of the local dialect is that— unlike Liverpudlians and Geordies, who revel in the way they speak —Ilkeston people tend to feel ashamed of their accent, and try and rid themselves of it wherever possible. The main reason for this is an obvious one, it being claimed by many that Ilkeston speech is just plain ugly! — well, that, of course, is a matter of opinion, but what is important is that this attitude has accelerated the process by which our dialects are becoming increasingly diluted, robbing our lives of yet a little more colour and variety, and severing us from our true heritage.

The somewhat simplified spellings we've devised come as close as we can get them to the sound pattern of Ilkeston speech, without becoming completely impossible to interpret and pronounce. English spelling itself, of course, is not phonetic, and involves compromises; we have simply added compromises of our own. Obviously it is impossible in print to capture the subtleties of spoken language, its 'music', its stresses and emphases. As an example of this, a lowland Scot could well say something like 'Ah canna wok wi' all that watter!' ('I cannot work with all that water'). In written form, an old Derbyshire miner would say what appears to be almost exactly the same thing, but if we heard them both there would be no difficulty in deciding which was the Englishman and which the Scot, because the 'music' of their speech would be completely different.

Little Miss Muffet

A Local Gleg at Nursery Rhymes

Humpty Dumpty

REGULAR FEATURES (1) OF THE EREWASH VALLEY DIALECT

The occasional idiosyncrasy — 'It's gerrin a bit black ower Bill's motha's' ('It looks as if it will rain'), for example—however striking and localized it may be, can never of itself give us a true understanding of the inner workings of a dialect.

A comprehensive picture of Ilkeston dialect will only emerge once we have considered, firstly (Part One) the way in which words are pronounced, and secondly (Part Two) the grammatical patterns which give it a special flavour and distinguish it from Standard English.

It is not 'rules' we are trying to establish, nor would we claim that every speaker's dialect exhibits all the features we mention. Whether we take a broad view or examine the speech of any individual speaker, there are inconsistencies everywhere, which is as it should be when we are discussing language.

All we seek to do, then, is to draw a broad sketch-map of the territory, as it were, leaving the details to be filled in by every speaker of 'Ilson'; hopefully every local reader will recognise here some of the language which he or she uses, or hears others use. The authors would appreciate any additions, corrections, or suggestions which might help make this record of a dialect as accurate as possible; for it to succeed, it must have its roots in the realities of everyday speech.

PRONUNCIATION
(or: 'It ain't what you say, it's the way that you say it'.)

There may be many reasons why any given person pronounces sounds in the way that he does; his age will affect his voice, so will his build, the state of his health, the way in which he imitates the people he thinks worth imitating, and even the climate in which he lives (it is no coincidence that people living in Liverpool, for instance, prone as they may be to catarrh in that rather damp climate, speak in a very nasal way).

One of the most formative influences upon pronunciation, however, will be the region in which a person lives; pronunciation, in fact, is a safer guide to dialect boundaries than the dialect itself, since accents are less readily borrowed from one region to another than dialectal words and phrases are.

What follows is a brief survey showing the ways in which local pronunciation differs from standard speech patterns.

Vowels: 'u' and 'a' sounds

Vowel sounds convey less information than the consonants which they separate, but it is the vowels, above all, that make any regional pronunciation distinctive. This is especially true of the full 'u' and short 'a' sounds which, more than any others, distinguish 'Northern' English from Southern Standard English.

The Full 'u'

In Ilkeston the 'u' in words like 'bus', 'custom', and 'sun' is always a full one (an 'uh' sound) as in 'Northern' English.

So: 'love' becomes 'luv', 'son' becomes 'sun', etc.

There are only three important exceptions to this rule: the words 'mother', 'bugger', and 'come' may be pronounced 'motha', 'bogger', and 'com' — a more traditional pronunciation than the alternative 'muther', 'bugger', and 'cum'. ('com', incidentally, may mean either 'come', 'came', or 'comb'!)

Attempts to 'correct' an Ilkeston dialect may lead the unwary speaker into difficulties. The fact is that the full 'u' sound has survived in Standard English, but is used much less frequently than in Ilkeston speech, and usually before an 'l' — 'pull', for example. It is not uncommon to hear a person from the North or Midlands, in an attempt to eradicate the full 'u' sound completely, use a 'posh u' where a Standard English speaker would use a full one — in the word 'butcher', for instance.

The short 'a'

The 'a' sound in words like 'after', 'plaster', 'grass', 'ask', 'laughter', 'bath', etc., is always the older short version.[1]

(It is perhaps too easy to assume that this short or flat 'a' never finds its way into the speech of the country's leaders and social élite. This is certainly not always the case: Edward VIII, announcing his abdication on the radio, pronounced the word 'broadcast' with a short 'a'; in the nineteenth century, Lord Curzon, later Viceroy of India, kept his Derbyshire 'a', and once gave instructions at the Foreign Office concerning an ornamental ink-well: 'Remove that object of glass and brass, and bring me alabaster!'; at least three English Prime Ministers in the nineteenth century, Gladstone, Sir Robert Peel and the Earl of Derby, used short 'a's, and a Lancashire accent. There were certainly mixed reactions in 1941, when Wilfred Pickles was asked to read the news on radio, and talked of 'aircraft carriers' — some people even thought the news broadcast was a hoax!)

Two exceptions to the short 'a' rule are 'half' and 'father', which traditionally are pronounced 'ayf' and 'fayther'.

---

1. The long 'a' is a relative newcomer to the language, not becoming fully established in Standard speech until the eighteenth century.

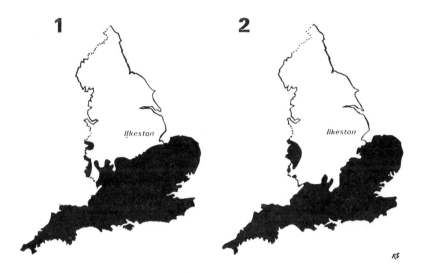

1

2

Ilkeston

Ilkeston

RS

Map 1: *The white region shows the approximate area of England in which a short 'a' is used (in a word like 'grass', for example). In the black Southern area, a variety of vowels would be used, ranging from a Standard South-Eastern 'ar' sound, to a West Country 'aah' sound.*

Map 2: *The white region shows the approximate area of England in which a full 'u' sound would be used (in a word like 'bus'). Note that here the border line is generally much further South than that on Map 1. This means that in an appreciable part of the South Midlands, a full 'Northern' 'u' vowel is used in conjunction with a long Southern 'a' sound.*

Other variations on the letter 'a'

The Standard English pronunciation of a word like 'Albany' (the 'Al' being pronounced as if it were 'All') is replaced by a more rational version, in which 'Al' is made to rhyme with 'pal'. On the other hand, the standard pronunciation of the vowel in words like 'alter', 'fault', and 'false' (again, an 'or' sound) gives way to a 'Northern' version: 'olter', 'folt', 'folse'.

The vowel sound in words like 'water', 'want', and 'swan' is sometimes given its traditional value, thus becoming — as in Shakespearian English—'watter', 'wannt' and 'swann'. ('Wash' and 'watch', however, become 'wesh' and 'wetch').

'Have' becomes 'ay'.

'Shake' becomes 'shek'; 'great' becomes 'gret'; 'make' becomes 'mek' (or 'ma'e'); 'take' becomes 'tek' (or 'ta'e').

(For 'day' becoming 'dee', etc., see next section on 'e' sounds).

A tendency in the traditional speech of this area which has almost entirely died out today, was that of pronouncing words which contain a short 'a' as if they were spelt with an 'o'. Thus, for instance, 'rat' became 'rot', 'man' became 'mon', etc.

21

Other Vowels

'e' sounds:

The long 'ee' sound often becomes an 'ay' sound. Thus 'green' becomes 'grain'; 'seen' becomes 'seyn'; 'speak' becomes 'speyk'; 'these' becomes 'thaise'; 'please' becomes 'plaise', etc.

(One noteable exception here is 'week', which becomes 'wick').

Notice, however, that this also works in reverse — so that 'ay' sounds become 'ee' sounds!

So, 'rain' becomes 'reen'; 'gate' becomes 'geet'; 'day' becomes 'dee', etc.,

Hence the well-known sayings:

'Eh kney/ed on a neel an' ot is kney!' or 'Dahn aar pit wey've got wails an' cheens.'

The short 'e' sound in a word like 'yet' is often changed, to become 'yit'; 'every' becomes 'ivry'; 'yesterday' becomes 'yisterdee'; 'never' becomes 'niver' (or 'neyer', as in 'Neyer mind!').

Again there is a reversal process at work here, since the vowel in a word like 'sit' sometimes changes, to produce 'set', as in: 'Set yersen dahn!'

'i' sounds:

The 'i' sound in a word like 'right' is frequently given an 'ay' sound: 'raight'. Thus, for example: 'frightened' becomes 'fraightened' (or 'frit'); 'light' becomes 'laight' ('Ay yuh gorra laight, yothe?') etc.

(A word of warning: certain words do not follow this pattern: 'might', 'knight', 'bite', 'kite').

'o' sounds:

The 'oh' sound in a word like 'over' is frequently shortened to produce 'ova' (though this is sometimes pronounced 'ower').

So, 'home' becomes 'om' (or 'wom') and 'open' becomes 'oppen'.

The 'oh' sound at the end of a word like 'window' is replaced by an 'er' sound, becoming 'winder'; 'pillow' becomes 'piller'; 'follow' becomes 'foller'; 'tomorrow' becomes 'temorrer', etc.

The open 'oh' sound in words like 'so' and 'go' become closed: 'soo', 'goo'. (The word 'going' can either be rendered as 'gooin' or 'gauin'; the word 'goes' becomes 'guz').

Just as local traditional speech reverses the 'ee' and 'ay' and the short 'e' and short 'i' sounds, so it also reverses the 'o' sounds, too. The closed 'o' sound is often pronounced open, 'oo' becoming 'oh' or 'ow': 'shoot' becomes 'showt'; 'two' becomes 'tow'; 'do' becomes 'doe' (or 'dow'); 'soon' becomes 'sone' (or 'sown'); and 'lose' becomes 'loze' (a pronunciation which is closer to the actual spelling, of course, than the Standard English version, 'looze').

If we bear in mind that at one time the standard pronunciation for words like 'book' and 'look' was 'buke' and 'luke', then the local variants, 'boke'/'bowk' and 'loke'/'lowk' may be seen as being consistent with this general pattern we have just outlined. (This does not mean that the 'uke' pronunciations are never used locally; on the contrary, with some dialect speakers they would crop up as frequently as would these 'oke'/'owk' alternatives).

There are some noteable exceptions, but generally speaking these reversal processes are becoming increasingly less common. Nevertheless, they are, in truth, a distinctive and remarkable feature of the more traditional Erewash Valley dialect.

To continue with 'o' sounds:

The vowel sound in words like 'now', 'town', etc., is usually pronounced nowadays with an open 'aah' sound: 'nah', 'tahn'. Similarly, 'south' becomes 'sahth'; 'house' becomes 'aase'; 'out' becomes 'aht'; 'cow' becomes 'caa'; 'found' becomes 'fahnd' (or 'fun').

This open vowel sound was less common a couple of generations ago, and older people, especially, may still be heard using a more closed sound, approximating to 'air'. Thus, 'town' becomes 'tairn'; 'about' becomes 'abairt', etc.

Words which contain an 'ol' are usually pronounced in Ilkeston speech as if the 'l' were not present: 'soldier' becomes 'sowjer'; 'shoulder' becomes 'showder'; 'old' becomes 'owd', etc., ('owd', of course, can also mean 'hold', as in: 'Owd yer ossesl').

'er' sounds:

Traditionally, words like 'bird' and 'shirt', which contain an 'er' sound, were usually pronounced 'bod' and 'shot'. Increasingly, however, an intermediate vowel is used — an 'air' sound.

Standard English	Modern Ilkeston	Traditional Ilkeston
Learn	Lairn	Lon
Dirty	Dairty	Dotty
First	Fairst	Fost
Third	Thaird	Thod
Whirled	Wairled	Woled
Word	Waird	Wod
World	Wairld	Wold
Worse	Wairse	Woss
Burst	Bairst	Bost
Curse	Cairse	Coss
Curtains	Cairtains	Cottins
Further	Fairther	Fother
Purse	Pairse	Poss
Turkey	Tairkey	Tockey
Turn	Tairn	Ton

This vowel shift is summed up by a conversation overheard on Ilkeston Market Place:

'A'm gooin te wok, nah then, yothe!'

"Wok!' Wot kind o' talk's that? Yo mean 'wairk' don't yuh?'

(Notice that there are exceptions to this general pattern: for example, 'occured' has only one alternative pronunciation, 'occaired'; the same is true of 'perfect', which becomes 'pairfect').

'or' sounds:

Words containing an 'or' sound which is in fact spelt 'augh' or 'ough', such as 'bought' and 'caught', are sometimes given the traditional pronunciation, whereby the 'or' becomes 'oh'.

Thus: 'bought' becomes 'bote'; 'thought' becomes 'thote'; 'taught' becomes 'tote', 'daughter' becomes 'dohter', etc.

The word 'Thee':

Before we leave vowel sounds, it is worth remembering that the single pronunciation, 'thee', can be used in local speech to represent any one of three completely different words:

1. 'They'; as in: 'Will thee?', 'Thee will!' (follows the 'nail' becomes 'neel' pattern).

2. 'There'; as in: 'Is thee a bus at ten o'clock?' or: 'Not much roam in ere, is thee?'

3. 'They're' ('They are'); as in: 'Yo canna say thee elegant!' (or, if you want to stress a different word, you can use the variation: 'Yo canna say *they* elegant!').

(Notice also: 'There's' becomes 'Thuz' or 'Thiz', as in: 'Loke! thuz undreds on 'em!' or: 'Thiz summat funny gooin off ere!').

Diphthongs

We have studied vowels in some detail, but must add one or two comments on the use of diphthongs. In simple terms, the word 'diphthong' describes the process whereby we begin pronouncing one vowel sound in a word, and end up with another.

In Standard English, 'new' contains a diphthong; we begin with 'ee', and finish with 'oo'. In Ilson speech, however, the first part of this operation is dispensed with, and we get a pure vowel sound: 'noo'. Similarly, 'Duke' becomes 'Dook' (or 'Doke'); 'stupid' becomes 'stoopid' (or 'stowpid'); 'Tuesday' becomes 'Toosdee' (or 'Toesdee'); 'beautiful' becomes 'bootiful' (or 'boatiful'); 'few' becomes ':foo', etc.[2]

Conversely, the almost imperceptible diphthong in the standdard pronunciation of words like 'where' and 'there' may sometimes be exaggerated rather than done away with, to produce 'weer' and 'theer'. Similarly, words like 'door' and 'floor', for example, may be pronounced 'dooer' and 'flooer'.

These diphthongized versions used in this area—'weer', 'theer', and so on — are close to traditional English speech; it is Standard English which has changed. There is, however, another set of local

2. Actually, far from avoiding the diphthong in the word 'few', a full dialect speaker would be more likely to exaggerate it: 'feeow'. In the same way, 'view' becomes 'veeow'.

non-standard diphthongs — most of them, probably, more recent in origin[3] — which seem to form part of a sub-dialect all its own: for example, 'wee-ak' for 'week', 'co-at' for 'coat', and 'me-an' for 'mean'. This kind of speech is frequently dismissed as 'Cotmanhay talk', and may even be carefully avoided by 'traditional' speakers, who, themselves, would be more likely to use the older pronunciations: 'wick', 'coot' and 'main'. Be that as it may, no survey of Ilkeston dialect would be complete without some reference to this type of speech, and below is a brief list of some common examples: 'afternoo-un' ('afternoon'); 'clo-uz' ('clothes'); 'cre-um' ('cream'); 'doh-unt' ('don't'); 'froo-ut' ('fruit'); 'Joo-un' ('June'); 'no-ut' ('note'—i.e., 'nothing'); 'ro-ud' ('road').

So much for vowels and diphthongs; we must now turn our attention to consonants.

Consonants: the letter 'h'

The letter 'h' is never pronounced in Ilkeston dialect: "eavy'; "ammer'; "itch 'ikin'; 'th 'orn o't'th'unter is 'eard ont th'ill.'

This is not necessarily a lazy form of speech, however. A Cockney speaker drops his 'h' to make life easier, and runs everything together, for example: 'ten an'arf'. Many Ilkeston speakers, on the other hand, would make a deliberate pause before the last word. Indeed, they have to work harder than the speaker of Standard English, because they close off the sound abruptly before the word "arf' (it's called a 'glottal stop'). So: 'ten an' a-arf' (listen carefully for just such phrases at local supermarket check-out counters). This kind of brief but definite pause gives local speech its characteristic jerky, staccato rhythm: 'a 'ead'; 'a 'orse'.[4]

Notice similar pauses in other phrases, too: 'Ah spoilt-it' (In Standard English, the 't' is carried over).

'Ah cun see it in yuh-eyes' (Standard English would run 'your eyes' together).

'Tek me te-Ilson' (Standard English would make a 'w' sound between 'to' and 'Ilson').

Very few dialects do contain a pronounced 'h', except for emphatic use — some Northern and East Coast areas are an exception — and in the eighteenth century it was fashionable to drop the 'h' even in Standard English. Even Americans talk today of thyme and parsley as "erbs'.

In any event, there is no need to worry about the 'h'; there is always the risk of it cropping up where it isn't wanted:

3. 'Recent', of course, is a comparative term; some of these diphthongs may, in fact, be more than two hundred years old, and it is just possible that these alternative pronunciations may stem from the migration to Ilkeston of a group of workers from another area, many generations ago.

4. Cockney may not use a glottal stop in the example quoted, but it is notable, like the Ilkeston accent, for its frequent use of this feature, usually to replace a 't' or a 'k' between vowels: 'toma'o'; 'pac'et', or even. 'Ho' wa'er bo'le' ('Hot water bottle').
   Even in Manchester, a local dialect speaker may be heard lamenting his football team's failure in a phrase rich in glottal stops: 'Wha' a pi'y Ci'y lost!'

'Ah'd like a hegg fer breakfast.'

It should be mentioned, before we leave the 'h', that it is omitted even if it comes in the middle, and not at the beginning, of a word: 'be'ind'; 'be'ave', 'ma'ogany', etc.

The word 'the':

It is not only the letter 'h' which is not pronounced in Ilkeston; one or more letters are frequently dropped in the word 'the', too. The general rule is to abbreviate 'the' to 't' before a consonant — to join it, in fact, to the word which precedes it: 'Ah wunna goo int' car'; 'Walk ont' causey!'; 'Eh wer dahn byt' side o't' road'; 'A'm not gooin intert' watter!'[5]

Before a vowel, the abbreviation becomes 'th': 'Th' oss-muck wall'; 'Th' animal tamer'.

So, in combination, you might have: 'Th' ole int' wall'. Sometimes, for good measure, both the 't' and 'th' forms are used together to represent a single 'the' — probably for ease of pronunciation: 'Are yuh gooin' intert' th' Arrer?' (a famous pub on Bath Street).

(Sometimes the 't' is replaced by a 'd', thus: 'Ah've bin lokin all ova d'place fer yo!' or: 'Dunna lay theer wid winder oppen!').

Other letters omitted:

No other letter is completely omitted in the way that 'h' is; certain other letters vanish occasionally, however, usually at the end of a word:

'ce' is left out in 'sin' ('since'),

'k' is left out in 'asses' ('asks'); 'masses' ('masks'); 'ma'e' ('make'); 'ta'e' ('take').

't' is left out in 'kep' ('kept') and 'lasses' ('lasts') — 'las'year' can even become: 'lash year'.

'd' is frequently left out in a phrase like: 'yo an' mey'.

'v' is left out in 'gi'e' ('give').

'th' is left out in 'wi' ('with'); sometimes pronounced as 'wee'. Also: 'wi'aht' ('without').

'l' is often omitted from 'only', to produce 'owny', and is also frequently left out in 'a'raight' ('all right') and 'a'ready' ('already').

'g' is normally left out of words ending in '-ing': 'walkin'', 'talkin''.

(For the record, some local speakers, far from not'pronouncing a 'g' at the end of a word, will sound it very clearly indeed, turning it into a hard 'g' which is stressed: 'sitting'; 'tongue'. This feature, in fact, is generally much more common in the North than in the East Midlands).

5. Frequently, this 't' is not sounded strongly — it is more of a shut-off noise than a pronounced sound; indeed, it is often difficult to detect the presence of the definite article at all, particularly where it is followed by a 't' or a 'd': 'ont' table'; 'int' dog-aase'.

'f' may be omitted in the word 'of', a feature especially noticeable before a vowel, when a glottal stop becomes necessary: 'a box o'oringes'; 'lots o'apples'.

'n' is frequently omitted in the word 'an' (the indefinite article). In other words, many Ilkeston speakers do not change the 'a' to an 'an' before a vowel, but use a glottal stop instead: 'a egg'; 'a animal', etc.

's' is omitted in certain plurals, for example: 'thotty year' agoo'; tow paand' o' apples', etc.

'w' is passed over in: 'backuds' ('backwards'); 'forruds' ('forwards'); 'allus/alluz' ('always'); 'awkud/ockud' ('awkward').

Words ending in 't' or 's' — the Intrusive 'r':

Where a word should end in 't' or 's', and is then followed by a vowel, the last letter is often omitted, and an 'r' substituted. So we have phrases like: 'Gerrup!'; 'Is tharall?'; 'Ah fegorrit'; 'A'd like te cum, burra canna.'; 'Burroo worrit?'; 'Eh purris 'at on' . . .

So, after a disastrous game of cricket, a batsman might say: 'Worraninnins!' (Notice, also, that sometimes a 't' becomes an 'r' even within a word — so 'better' can become 'berrer').

Perhaps the most frequently-heard example of this 'Intrusive 'r'' is the local version of the Standard English farewell salute; 'ta-tar!' becomes 'tarrar!' or even 'trar!' (Interestingly enough, where there *is* an 'r' present already in Standard English, it may not be pronounced in Ilson: 'on your own' becomes 'on yuh-own'.)

Stresses:

A final word on pronunciation: pronouncing the right sounds isn't enough; talking 'Ilson' involves knowing which *part* of a word needs to be stressed.

Variations from Standard English include: 'A'ver*ti*ser' (Standard English: '*Ad*vertiser'); '*Neck-lace*' (Standard English: '*Neck*-lace'); 'The Cw*op*' (Standard English: 'The *Co*-op'); 'Winter*time*' (Standard English: '*Winter*time'); 'comm*ent*' (Standard English: '*Comm*ent'); '*con*fuse' (Standard English: 'con*fuse*'); 'th'*ead*master' (Standard English: 'the head*master*').

PUB TALK

HAVE DONKEY WILL TRAVEL

Wen anybody wannts te talk te mey, thi've got te talk English . . .
I ad no int'rest in French ut skowell. I ad no intention o'gooin te
France . . . ah've not nah . . . unless it's wee BEF or summat. D-day
landins, that's th'owny time yo'll sey mey theer! Ah wouldna goo
up int th'eer . . . not on a plane, neow! Ah wouldna goo ont watter!
Dunna mind trains . . . D'yo know, yuh know thaise ere funny facts
yuh raid abaht . . . ther wer one, an it's true, ah dunna know aah . . .
thuz more folks int wold killed be donkeys than thee is in aircrashes!
True! . . . true! It saims impossib!e, burrit's true!

TIGER NUTS AN'
LICORISH STICKS

Wey'd gerrup Sundee mornin
An' gerron aht te plee,
It wer stow pot fer yer breakfast
An bread an lard fer tea.
If yer owd man shaated yuh
Yo dossn't stay on aht.
Yuh knew yo'd ay te dab on in
Or else yo'd gerra claat.
Mi mam wer allest wokkin,
So wey kept aht on er wee,
Wey'd clear off dahn inter t'failds
An sum raight good games wey'd plee.
Or sumtimes wey'd stay int strait
An gerrusens inter a faight.
Wey'd plee under Dobba's winder
Wen eh wer still 'a-kip',
So eh'd chuck summat at us,
An wey would ay sum lip.
Soon ud cum Mundee mornin
An off te skewl wey'd goo.
But sumtimes ah'd goo dahn te t'faild
Thinkin nubdee ud know
Till t'skewl bobby tonned up ut om,
Ah din't know wot te do!
Mi fayther belted mey that naight,
Till mam said, 'Gi'e ower, Jack!'
That belt din't ayf cum keen yuh know,
Eh nearly brok me back!
Wen Thozdee cum
Wey'd wait fer dad
Eh'd gi'e us a ayp'ny
That's all wey ad.
Wey'd goo dahn t'shop
Weer t'tuffies wer good
Tiger nuts, an chewin wood
Wey din't ay much in them theer dees
But wey grew up better in so many wees.
All me mates smile wen wey think o't'past,
Wey did sum raight things an we ad sum raight laffs.
Things ave all changed in many a wee
An note's t'same in Ilson tedee!

TYNA BELFIELD

QUIZ

TEST YOURSELF

Here are some typical local expressions — see if you can 'decipher' them. (We've made them deliberately a bit more tricky by running several words together).

Then rate yourself: Full marks — you've got a twisted mind, or you've cheated. Half marks — read this book and try again. No marks — move to London.

Clues are given in brackets. (Answers on page 48).

1. **ISITIZEN?** (A question of ownership).
2. **TINTAAN!** (A statement about ownership).
3. **SUPWIYO?** (A slightly hostile question).
4. **ASTADAWESH?** (Can also be hostile; could be mother talking to child).
5. **YOWLKOPPIT!** (Possibly a response to a negative answer to No. 4).
6. **ITSTONNINTUREEN** (The weather).
7. **ARKATTIT!** (The weather—it's now raining).
8. **OOWOREEWEE?** (The sort of question a wife might ask of a bar-maid concerning her husband's whereabouts).
9. **WORREEWEEISSEN?** (Another question to the bar-maid).
10. **AYAGORRAWEEYA?** (The question the wife asks the husband once she's found him).
11. **AIRBAIRTMEY?** (Asked by a person who has found himself left out of a round or drinks).
12. **AWICKATHOZDEE** (A future appointment).
13. **AYENNYONYAOTTYA?** (Father to his many children after they've fallen off a swing).
14. **YONORRAYINNOTUFFIES!** (Mother's first reaction to her child who is howling for sweets).
15. **THEMSGOODUNSINTEM?** (Mother has given in; she eats one of the sweets herself, and likes them).
16. **GIZZAYFONIT!** (Mother has become hooked on the sweets; she wants her child to share his last one with her).
17. **AIRTHIKAYPIN?** (Friendly greeting).
18. **AREYUHGUNNACORLUNAYAJAR?** (An invitation to the pub).
19. **AYAGORRITRAYT?** (We're asking how you've made out with the quiz).
20. **ARCANNAMAYNOWTONIT!** (This is probably your reply to our question).

30

REGULAR FEATURES (2) OF THE EREWASH VALLEY DIALECT

GRAMMATICAL FEATURES

If you ever wanted, as a non-native, to learn to speak 'Ilson', you would need to do more than just acquire a lot of new vocabulary; calling brussels sprouts 'nobby greens' will not in itself convince anyone that you were born and bred within the sound of St. Mary's church bells.

Dialects — and those of Ilkeston and the Erewash Valley are no exception — usually make remarkably free use of the rules of standard grammar; or, to be more accurate, a regional dialect obeys traditional grammatical rules of its own. 'Correctness' is not an issue: speakers of 'Ilson' are not trying to speak Standard English and failing. They are adhering, more or less strictly, to a grammar which, like the Ilkeston accent, has its own pedigree — indeed, the grammatical structure of many dialects is closer to Elizabethan English than to Modern Standard English.

Just as vowels have a central supporting function in words, so verbs are vital to the structure of sentences. We shan't make very much sense of verbs in isolation, however, and first a word or two needs to be said about pronouns, since they relate the verbs to the speaker and to other people or things.

The pronunciation of Ilkeston speech — its accent — has already been dealt with at length in Part One; it will be useful, however, at the risk of repetition, to begin with a word or two about how pronouns are pronounced locally:

'I'. Nowadays the first person singular pronoun is usually pronounced something like 'Ah'.[1] Traditionally, it was once more of a closed sound: 'Ar'. The exception to this pronunciation is where the verb following begins with a vowel, in which case 'I' is used. (for example: 'I axed im if ee wer alraight.')

'You'. This becomes 'yuh' or 'yo', depending upon the emphasis: '*Yuh* canna com in ere', but '*Yo* not commin!'

Nowadays, unfortunately, the forms 'thou' (subject) and 'thee' (object) have all but disappeared from everyday Ilkeston speech. They were once commonly used in this area — and in Derbyshire dialects generally — especially down the pits. The way in which these forms are pronounced follows a general rule of pronunciation: 'Thou' usually becomes 'Tha' or 'Thaa'; 'Thee' commonly becomes 'They', and 'Thy' becomes either 'Thi' or 'Thaa' depending upon the emphasis: 'Weer's *thi* cap?', or 'It's *thaa* goo'.

(Historically, 'thou', 'thee', 'thy' and 'thine' — this last form very rarely heard in Ilkeston, if at all — were the usual singular

---

1. This may become shortened or lengthened according to the context: 'A'm commin!', but, 'Aah dunna know!'

pronouns. During the Middle English period (c.11th—14th centuries), the plural forms, 'ye' (subject) and 'you' (object), slowly replaced the older pronouns in singular use, first in very formal usage, then almost altogether. The subject form 'ye', though still used in the Authorized Version of the Bible in 1611, then also died out. Modern English only retains 'thou' and its variants in some dialects, where its use is normally a friendly one. (This makes English unusual in Modern European languages, since French ('tu'), German ('du'), and Spanish ('tu'), for example, all have two separate singular forms, familiar and formal).

'He': this becomes 'eh' or 'ee'. (Thus following a general rule of pronunciation, including, of course, the 'No H' rule).

'She': there are two possible variations here:
(a) 'Oh' This is the full dialect version. It is descended from Old English ('heo'), and is similar to the Scandinavian forms found in other Northern dialects (e.g. the 'hoo' form of Lancashire). In the ninth century, Ilkeston itself was, of course, part of the Danelaw, which included Derby as one of its five boroughs.
(b) 'Shey'. This follows a general rule of pronunciation, and is rather similar to the Mediaeval 'Standard English' pronunciation.

'We' — pronounced 'wey', and follows a general rule of pronunciation. ('Wey', incidentally, can mean 'we' or 'we are').

'They'. Usually becomes 'thee' (see section on pronunciation). Variations include:
'Thee not cumin, are *thee?'* ('They're not coming, are they?')
'They not cumin, are *thee?'* ('They're not coming, are they?')
(The words 'they' and 'them' did not exist in Old English, but are loan words from the Scandinavian).

So much for the basic subject pronouns and their pronunciation.

In local dialect use, pronouns are frequently used in non-standard ways:

1. Object Pronouns
The object form of a pronoun will be heard instead of the subject, usually in a question:
'Weer is 'er?' 'Is 'er ready yit?' (''er' for 'she')
'Is 'em oppen yit?' (''em' for 'they')
'Should us?' ('us' for 'we')
In the negative, this becomes:
'In't 'em?' ('Aren't they?')
(Note also: 'Gi'us a bite/giz a bite' ('us' for 'me') — this is common in very many dialects).

An object pronoun may also replace the subject form in the following instances, where there is a certain demonstrative flavour to the sentence:
'Oo worrit?'
''*im* wit' Rolls' (*'He/that man* with the Rolls Royce')

or:

'Oo took it?'

''*er* wit' gloves on' ('*She/that woman* with the gloves on')

2. Possessive Pronouns (and adjectives)

Possessive adjectives and possessive pronouns are often non-standard in Erewash Valley dialect.

The object pronoun 'us/uz' is very commonly heard for the possessive adjective 'our' — a feature usually declared by Dialect Surveys to be present only in North Derbyshire.

'Wey gooin fer uz dinners' ('We're going for our dinner')

Where 'our' does not become 'uz', it is usually pronounced 'aar', as in the following: (Note the non-standard word order!)

'Mey'n aar kid'll com wee yuh!'

Similarly, the object form 'me' is often heard for the possessive adjective 'my' — though whether this results merely from a slight variation in pronunciation is hard to determine:

'Weers me ankychief?'

Other alternative pronunciations, depending upon the context, or stress, or importance of the following word, are:

'Giz *mi* cap!'; 'Are yuh gooin' *maa* road?' or 'Ello *ma* duck!'

(Note here the close parallel with the different forms for 'thy': 'thi cap', '*thaa* road'.)

Ilkeston speech makes use of a traditional set of possessive pronouns, in which the final 's' is replaced by an 'n'. (Perhaps by analogy with 'mine' and 'thine', or perhaps meaning 'his-one', 'our-one' etc.)

e.g. 'Ah didna know it wer *yorn*' ('yours')

'Is it *izzen?*' ('his')

'No, its *airn*' ('hers')

'Laive that, it's *aan!*' ('ours')

'That's *theirn*, soo dunna tuch it!' ('theirs')

3. Demonstrative Pronouns (and adjectives)

Just as the object pronoun 'us' is used for the possessive adjective 'our', so the object pronoun 'them' is used in place of 'those':

(a) As a demonstrative adjective:

'Ah wannt *them* bokes'

(b) As a demonstrative pronoun:

'Gi'me *them* ova theer'

The emphatic forms, 'This 'ere', 'these 'ere', 'that there', and 'them there' usually replace the simple demonstratives: 'this', 'these', 'that', and 'those'.

4. Relative Pronouns

The word 'wot' ('what') replaces the relative pronouns 'which', 'who', or 'whom'.

'That comic *wot* ah read' ('which')

'That man *wot* passed me' ('who')

'That gel *wot* ah saw' ('whom')

The word as ('uz') may similarly be used as a relative pronoun:
"im *uz* limps'; 'er *uz* speaks posh' ('who').

(Eliza Doolittle. in 'Pygmalion', having been taught to speak immaculate Standard English, still found problems with: 'Them *as* done 'er in').

The use of 'as' here is probably more common than 'what' in the traditional dialect of this area.

5. Reflexive Pronouns

It is usual in traditional Ilson speech for 'sen' (from Middle English 'seluen') to replace 'self' in the reflexive pronouns. The Northern form is 'sel'; 'sen' is the North Midland form.

So: 'Plaise yersens'; 'Plaise thisen'; 'Eh did it is-sen', etc. (The use of one basic form, 'sen' or 'sens', is simpler and more economical, of course, than the Standard English variations, 'self' and 'selves').

There is no total consistency here, however: sometimes 'self' or 'selves' is retained:

'Eh asked is-self' ('his-self')

'They asked the-selves' ('their-selves')

There is a remarkable rationalization in operation here, evident whether 'self' or 'sen' is used. Standard English reflexive pronouns are inconsistent, in that they all employ a possesive form — 'my' 'thy', 'its', 'our', 'your' — except for the third person singular and plural, where an object form is used: 'him', 'them'. This local dialect — in common with many others — removes this inconsistency, by using the possessive form for the third person singular and plural — 'his-self' and 'their-selves' — thus bringing these into line with all the others.

Shortened versions exist, too; the familiar cry on local buses: 'Owd yer tight!' is a simplification of 'Owd yersens/selves tight!' Similarly, 'Sit thi dairn' is a shorter variation on 'Sit thisen dairn' or 'Sit yersen dairn'.

(Note that 'Owd yerselves tight' or 'Sit yersen dairn' are, in any case, dialectal in construction; the Standard English imperative form is shorter, and uses no reflexive pronoun: 'Hold tight!' or 'Sit down (please)').

Other shortened versions include:

'Ay yuh weshed *yuh?*' ('yourself').

'Ah dressed *me*' ('myself').

(Here the simple object pronoun replaces the reflexive pronoun).

6. Indefinite Pronouns

There are special forms of the indefinite pronouns in Ilkeston speech:

(a)   'Note' (Standard English, 'nothing'; but Standard English does have 'nought', which nowadays is usually reserved for the figure 'zero').

So: 'It's woth note!' (Notice also the adverbial use: 'It's note extraordin'ry) or, in a double negative: 'Ah've ad no dinner nor note!'

Alternatively, you may hear a phrase like 'None burra cowd' ('Nothing but a cold').

(b) 'Ote' ('Anything' — Standard English archaic form: 'aught')
    So: 'It wer grand uz ote!'

(The pronunciation of these two words follows the local tradi- tional pattern already referred to in the section on pronunciation, whereby words containing an 'or' sound which is spelt 'augh' or 'ough' change this to an 'oh' sound. The pronunciations 'nowt' and 'owt' (the vowel sound rhyming with 'cow') belong to areas much further north than Ilkeston, as in the familiar Yorkshire maxim: 'If thee do owt fer nowt, do it fer thisen!')

(c) 'Summat' ('Something')
    So: 'Thiz summat up ere!'

VERBS

So much for pronouns; now a special mention must be made of verbs.

The verb 'to be', precisely because it is the most widely-used of all, exhibits a number of distinctive and non-standard forms in the local dialect. Sometimes a speaker will decline to use the verb itself at all.

In the present: 'Yo in a bittera 'urry' ('are' omitted).

In the present, using a negative: 'Yo not commin!' ('are' omitted).

In the future, using a negative: 'Eh not say ote' ('will' omitted).

In the future, using a negative question: 'Not ee elp yuh?' ('will' omitted) — or:

'Thar'll dow, norrit?' ('will' omitted).

Where a plural is involved, the use of the verb will often be covered by the use of the all-purpose words: 'Wey' and 'They':

'Wey raight!' ('We're all right!') or:

'They ignorant!' ('They're rude!').

It is a common feature of most dialects for the agreement between subject and verb to be non-standard; many West Country and West Midland dialects, for example, will use 'You'm' or 'We'm' for 'You are' or 'We are'.

Ilkeston speech is no exception; the plural form of the verb 'to be' in the past tense, 'were', is used with all subjects, singular or plural:

'Ah wer commin om'

'Eh wer waitin ont corner' (Question form: 'Worree?' — i.e. 'Were he?')

'Oh wer laffin'

'It wer reenin'

(Of course it is possible that these forms are in reality just a local pronunciation of 'was'!)

Ironically enough, the first and third person singular form of the past tense, 'was', is frequently only to be found in a question, in which the Standard English would be 'were'[1]:

'Was yuh wantin ote?'

(Social conventions, incidentally, may accept and then reject alternative forms of the verb: so in Trollope's novels concerning the Pallisers, it was very fashionable for the upper classes of the nineteenth century to use a plural form with a singular subject—'He don't', in place of 'He doesn't', for example.)

Equally, a singular form may be used with a plural subject: 'Thee int (i.e. isn't) many cakes left' ('There aren't') or the grammatically extraordinary: 'Them's good 'uns' ('They're'); or 'Is 'em?' ('Are they?')

The agreement of the future tense of the verb 'to be' causes problems even to speakers of Standard English, since both 'will' and 'shall' are reduced to ''ll' in speech, and thus the old distinction between the two words has become blurred.[2] Traditional Standard English grammar has 'shall' for the first person singular and plural, and 'will' for all other uses of the future tense (only complicated by the imperative use, also not strictly adhered to even by Standard English speakers, in which 'will' and 'shall' are reversed: 'I *will* go!'; 'You *shall* behave!' Hence the difficulties experienced by the drowning Frenchman, who cried: 'I will drown, and no-one shall save me!') A similar confusion exists, of course, with the forms 'should', (first person singular and plural) and 'would' (all others), which are reduced in speech to ''d'.

The only grammatical structure which demands that the speaker plump for 'shall' or 'will' or 'should' or 'would' is the question, where the verb is separated from its subject, and has to be voiced in full. It is common to hear such non-standard agreements in Ilkeston as 'Shall yuh cum?' or 'Shall yuh close the door, please?'

It is tempting to predict that the 'shall'/'will' and 'should'/'would' distinctions may well disappear from the spoken language altogether in due time, since even people who would like to make a distinction between them are not always certain how to make it, and the existence of the two separate forms has very little practical function, in any case.

Passing on, then, from the verb 'to be' and the agreement of subject and verb: another noticeable feature of local dialect is the substitution of one tense of the verb for another.

The present tense may be used for the past:

'Ah *com* ere yisterdee' ('*I came*')
'Eh *give* it me las wick' ('*He gave*')

The simple past form is sometimes used for a past participle:

'Oh's *ett* that cob' ('has eaten')
'Eh's *wrote* a letter' ('has written')

---

2. Notice, however, the very accurate abbreviated form sometimes heard around Ilkeston: 'Ah s'll' for 'I shall'.

'Oh's *fell* int watter' ('has fallen')
'Eh's *drank* it all!' ('has drunk')
'Oh's *trod* in sum mud' ('has trodden')
Equally, a past participle may be used for the simple past form:
'It *stunk*' ('stank')
'Wey *done* it' ('did')
'Ah *seen* im yisterdee' ('saw')
(Not to be confused with: 'Ah seen im threy times this wick', in which the Standard past participle, 'seen', is used, but without the auxiliary, 'have').

Most English verbs can be classified as 'weak' or 'strong', according to the way in which they form the past tense and past participle. Weak verbs add -ed, -d, or -t (walk/walked; love/loved; sleep/slept); strong verbs change their internal vowel (swim/swam teach/taught).

In Old English there were about three hundred and eighty strong verbs; in Modern English there are only about ninety which remain. Weak verbs, on the other hand, have increased enormously in number — and any new verbs which are added to the language are automatically conjugated in the weak fashion, which is easier, more consistent, and regular.

Several verbs which were once strong have become weak over a period of time — the past tense of 'to snow' for example, used to be 'snew' (commonly used by Chaucer) and the past tense of 'to dive' used to be 'dove', which is still used by American speakers.

Dialects frequently modify a strong verb for use as a weak one — thereby, in a sense, being ahead of their time in the rationalization and simplification of the language.

Ilson examples include the simple past forms:
'Ah *knowed* 'im' ('I knew')
'Ah *telled* 'im' ('I told')
'It *growed*' ('It grew')
Also:
'Ah *wakkened* up ut ayf past ten' ('I awoke'/'I woke up')
'Ah *catched* im wen ee com rahnd this mornin'' ('I caught')
and the past participles:
'Ah've *knowed* im ten year' ('I have known')
'Ah've *telled* yuh a undred times!' ('I have told')
'It's *growed*' ('It has grown')
By contrast, at least two verbs—'to give' and 'to seem'—are modified almost in the way that Standard strong verbs are, by having their internal vowel changed:
'It owny *sempt* like yisterdee' ('seemed')
or:
'Yuh *gen* me te' much' ('have given'); 'Wey'd abaht *gen* yuh up' ('had given'); 'Ah *gen* 'im a good idin'' ('gave').

Negatives

Standard English adds 'not' or 'n't' to a verb to form the negative; in traditional Erewash Valley dialect this is often contracted to 'na', sometimes accompanied by a slight change in the verb itself. Note that all the verbs in the following list may be used in conjunction with other verbs, that is, as auxiliaries, though each can also stand alone:

Asna (hasn't); anna (haven't); adna (hadn't); worna/wasna (wasn't); doesna (doesn't); dunna (don't); didna (didn't); isna/inna (isn't); mustna/munna (mustn't); shanna (shan't); willna (won't); nedna (needn't); canna (can't); couldna (couldn't); dossna (daren't); wouldna (wouldn't); etc.

Sometimes a modified form of these traditional negatives is used, so that, for example, 'wouldna' becomes 'wunt'; dossna' becomes 'dossn't'; 'anna' becomes 'ant' ('ant' can also mean 'hasn't'!); 'worna/wasna' becomes 'wornt' or 'wont'; 'isna/inna' becomes 'int',[3] and so on.

Not all speakers, of course, will use these more traditional forms; if not, they may well use an alternative construction which is equally non-standard.

Taking the future tense of the verb 'to be' as an example: 'I shall not' is the full written Standard form. Everyday spoken Standard English contracts this to 'I shan't'; Ilkeston speakers, by contrast, are as likely to say 'I'll not'. That is to say, the three words implied ('I shall not') are exactly the same in Standard English and the Erewash Valley; the only difference is the way in which these words are separated and abbreviated. So, similarly, 'He'll not' often replaces the Standard 'He won't' (but remember the alternative, 'Eh not', where 'will' is omitted completely, or the Ilson equivalent of the Standard 'It won't matter' — 'It not matter').

The same thing is true of the verb 'to have'; spoken Standard English has 'I haven't'/'I hadn't' and 'he hasn't'/'he hadn't'; Ilkeston speakers who do not use the traditional forms ('I anna'/'I adna' or 'eh asna'/'eh adna') will probably use the alternative: 'ah've not'/'ah'd not' and 'eh's not'/'eh'd not',

Finally, the double negative — common both in Shakespearian English and modern Cockney, for example — is frequently used in Ilkeston: 'I ant got none.' (for: 'I haven't got any').

Prepositions

In any language, it is the smallest and shortest of words — their form, and their inclusion or exclusion—which gives most difficulty to non-native speakers; this is especially true of prepositions, as any pupil who has struggled with the German language, or French expressions like 'se souvenir **de**' or 'rendre **à**' will testify.

Local dialect frequently uses prepositions in an unorthodox

---

3. Hence, 'It isn't in the tin' might appear in Ilkeston as something like: 'Tin-tin-tin!'

way. Sometimes, like verbs, they may be omitted completely:

'It belongs me' ('to' is omitted)

'Oh sent it me' ('to' is omitted)

'Ah live next 'Woolworths' ('to' is omitted)

'Owd a minute' ('on' is omitted)

'Oh wants 'er 'ead lookin' ('at' is omitted)

'Oh's gooin fer a teacher' (with the sense 'going *in* for teaching' or 'going to be a teacher').

Sometimes, by contrast, an extra or redundant preposition is included: consider a mother speaking to her young child who is walking along a wall:

'Gerrup off on it afore yuh fall!'

There are three prepositions in a row here, two of which, 'up' and 'on', are redundant. 'Off on' is a variation on the construction familiar in many dialects, 'off of', in which 'of' is redundant. 'Off on' is marginally more common than 'off of' before a vowel, but there is no consistent pattern here.

If prepositions are not omitted or added, they may be changed. The 'on' for 'of' substitution, mentioned above, is one of the commonest, and dates from the Middle English period:

'Sum *on* 'em's finished'; 'Gizzayfonit' ('Give me half of it'). Other substitutions include the following:

'*Agen* t'Police Station' ('Against', meaning 'next to')

'Wot's gooin *off?*' ('on')

'Sit *aside* mey!' ('beside')

'Not as ah know *to*' ('of')

'Wot d'yuh think *to* it?' ('of')

'I 'ate waitin *of* sumbody' ('for')

'Eh's fed up *of/on* 'er gooin' te Bingo' ('with')

That concludes most of the principal distinguishing features of the grammatical structure of Ilkeston speech; sharp-eyed readers will no doubt spot others in the glossaries. All that remains here is to mention a few more instances in which local usage differs from Standard English as far as parts of speech are concerned.

Adverbs may be omitted:

'Ah can't get' ('I can't get *there*', or: 'I can't make it')

Other adverbs may be shortened or changed:

'Wey'd berra do that *after*' ('We'd better do that *afterwards*')

'It's for sale *yet*' ('It's *still* for sale')

'Eh wer *that* poorly' ('He was *so* ill' or 'He was *really* ill' — an adverb of degree.)

(Compare: 'It's a nice day' — 'It is *that*' or 'It is *an* 'all')

Consider, too, the strange placing of the adverb, 'never', in the following example gleaned from a Marlpool man:

'Wey'd niver a faal' (We never had a fowl/chicken).

Adjectives may be changed:

'A fortnit *since*' ('A fortnight *ago*')

Notice also the comparative adjective, 'wairser' for 'worse' — the

Ilson version using a double comparison.

Conjunctions may be changed:

'Ah'll not be theer *wi'aht* (without) ah let yuh know' ('unless')

'Worree a staat pairson, *else* a thin 'un?' ('or')

(Perhaps, in this case, 'else' is a shortened version of 'or else')

'Wey knoo *uz aah* (as how) eh wouldna part wee is munny wi'aht a faight' ('as how' replaces the subordinating conjunction 'that')

In the nineteenth century, incidentally, a typical speaker of the Erewash Valley dialect would have substituted the word 'nor' for the subordinating conjunction, 'than': 'Ah'm a better man nor thee'.

Alternatively, an extra conjunction may be added, as in: '*Same* as ah say' ('*As* I say').

A final footnote should be added, concerning a particularly distinctive feature of Ilkeston speech. Just as some European languages repeat a word or phrase for emphasis, so it is common to hear such repetition in Ilkeston, stressing or emphasizing what is being said:

'They don't play cards, *they don't!*'

or

'Yo've gorra big gob, *yo ay!*'

or

'Ah like Westerns, *ah do!*'

or a slight variation:

'Eh's a raight 'un, *is Fred!*'

THE ILSON CROSS DRESSING

Well-dressings are still a common feature in several Derbyshire villages, but Ilkeston used to have its own cross-dressing, in which an antique stone cross which stood in the centre of the market place was decorated with oak boughs and a flag, surmounted by a little waxen figure called 'Charles in the oak'.

The Venerable Whitehead, writing of this annual festival in the 1850's, says that the base of this cross was still standing in the year 1809; it appears that not everyone behaved with suitable reverence on these occasions, and the worthy clergyman complains that 'these Cross Dressings were not without alloy of evil'. Fights were not uncommon, bull-baiting took place in the bull ring on Hunger Hill (now Nottingham Road) and cock-fighting was a favourite pastime. The redeeming features, however, included 'those matchless cakes yclept "spice cakes"', and a number of 'rustic games . . . peculiar to the neighbourhood', such as 'Will pegs' and 'Pricking the belt'.

"STEP IN KING GEORGE AND CLEAR THE WAY!"

THE ANCIENT MUMMERS' PLAYS OF ILKESTON

'Mumming' or 'masking' plays, at one time performed the length and breadth of England, are, like morris dancing, believed to be rooted deep in our distant pagan past. They were originally a symbolic spectacle of death and resurrection, and were performed by 'guisers' because of an ancient belief that if the players were recognised their magic power would be broken. There are many variations, but basically the plot as it has come down to us revolves around a fight between St. George or King George and an enemy (the Turkish Knight, Bold Slasher, Black Prince of Darkness etc.) One or other is killed and miraculously restored to life by the Doctor. This simple story symbolised the eternal conflict between good and evil, light and darkness, fertile spring and sterile winter — an expression of man's preoccupation with the cycle of the seasons.

At least three villages in the Ilkeston area — Kirk Hallam, Stanley and West Hallam — are known to have continued a tradition of 'guising' as part of their Christmas celebrations, certainly until the end of the nineteenth cenury, and, in the case of Stanley, until much later (c. 1920).

The Kirk Hallam play was collected some years ago from Mr James Carrier who went out with the mummers around the turn of the century. He remembered the excitement of getting the costumes ready a month before Christmas, with mothers and sisters helping to dress the characters in gay apparel made of coloured paper and cardboard. The party of young men made a round of the pubs, farms and houses in the Kirk Hallam area, and many a time there was over a pound each to be shared out at the end of an evening. Here is a short extract from the play, which contained six characters: First Guiser, King George, Young Turk, Princess of Paradise, the Doctor and Betsy Betsy Belzebub:

PRINCESS: *In comes Princess of Paradise, boldly I appear! I come to seek my only son, mine only son, he's bleeding here. Who did him kill? Who did him slay? Who caused his precious blood to spill?*

KING GEORGE: *I did him kill — I did him slay — I caused his precious blood to spill!*

PRINCESS: *Send for the £5 Doctor!*

CHORUS: *There ain't one.*

PRINCESS: Send for the £10 Doctor! (In comes £10 Doctor)

DOCTOR: My name is Doctor M. D. Brown, the finest Doctor in the town. I cure the hip, the grip — the grunts, the gout. I'll turn your belly inside out...

We have recently collected details of the Stanley play from Mr Alfred Harris who now lives in Ilkeston. Again, there were six characters: Open Door, King George, Little Turk, Little Turk's Mother, the Doctor and the Jolly Old Man. The party of mummers, wearing old clothes and with faces blackened with soot or black-lead, made a round of the village houses and pubs, always entering without knocking, and at the end of each performance consuming vast quantities of mince pies, pork pies and ale. Traditionally, these plays were passed on by word-of-mouth; collectors who have written them down have, understandably, done so in Standard English as we have here, but Mr Harris reminds us that they were originally performed in broad dialect.

Here are some of the opening lines of the Stanley play, spoken by 'Open Door', played by Mr Harris. In essence, all mumming plays begin in this way:

I open the door, I enter in,
I hope your favours I shall win:
Whether I sit, stand, lie or fall,
I'll do my duty to please you all...
Come, stir up the fire and make a light,
For in this house, there'll be a fight
If you don't believe the words I say,
Step in King George and clear the way!

Evidently, Mr Harris was kept very busy; not only was he involved in the mummers' play, but being a dark-haired lad, he was also Stanley's 'first footer'. Beginning around 5.30 on New Year's morning to catch the colliers before they lift for the pit, he would visit each house in turn to let the New Year in. Since each stop involved partaking of some liquid refreshment, his traditional greeting of 'A Happy New Year!' must have become somewhat slurred by the time he got to the end of his round!

Sadly, we were too late to collect full details of the West Hallam play, but Mrs Beryl Boddy, whose father, George Flint, was one of the performers, has remembered a few lines from it. The seven characters included, apparently, a 'Be-elzebub' noted for the skill and dexterity with which he twirled his club and dripping pan in the air. The play was last performed around 1890. Mr Flint, who played the Fool, wore moleskin trousers tied with 'yorks', a union flannel shirt, a hand-made smock and a straw hat with a fringed brim. Other characters were clad in smocks and corduroys. The Fool's opening lines were as follows:

Here comes I, who's never been yet,
With my big head and little wit.
My head is big, my wit is small,
I'm the biggest fool amongst you all!

Happily, these, and other, ancient folk plays are making something of a comeback, having been resurrected by several of the revival Morris sides in the area. It is comforting to think that after a break of more than fifty years, King George is once more

'...safe and sound;

As any man on England's ground'.

OOH, ARK UT MEY AGEN!

It seems that a local female celebrity was asked if she would care for another helping. Attempting to correct her earlier 'faux pas', she replied: 'Ho no, hi've 'ad a helegant sufficiency of hevery delicacy ...an' if hi 'ad hany more, hi should bost!'

(The story is probably apocryphal).

A TRIP DAIRN T'PIT

A TYPICAL COALING SHIFT THIRTY YEARS AGO

Here, Mr Ray Huthwaite of Cotmanhay describes what it was like to work on the coalface at Cossall Colliery during the late 1940's. Simply to reach his place of work was something of an ordeal:

Yo'd aye te scrozzle ower tubs n' jotties at geet end wi' pick, shovel, wringer, wedge, 'ommer, pairder tin, snap n' rammin', an' inter t'benk. Ah wer on panside thod length up. Mi clanny 'ud bey 'ingin' frum t'strop arairnd mi neck, an' ah'd ay te shimmy mi wee up pans te me owd length afore t'pans got gooin'. Ah'd gleg at rowf an' sey as it wor a'raight, gi'e it a thomp 'r tow wi'd pick, an' sey as it wor seef, then gerra cetch prop set afore ah started gummin' up.

Wen t'gummin' wor aht ud wee, ah'd 'oller fer t'shotfirer te blow fost 'ole.

Once at the back end of the coal, Mr Huthwaite's next task was to make a slot in which to insert his first wooden roof bar:

Wen yo'd got te'd backs, yo'd stomp airt fer'd fost split, an' ma'e sarten yo'd a prop sawed te t'raight length, then yo'd gi'e it sum 'ommer til it wor up.

The next stage in the operation was drilling for another shot:

Wey'd a owd 'and-waler wi' stand, worrum an' threy sets o'drills. Settin' up t'stand an' tonnin' t'th'andle in low benk wor a bit awkud, 'cos yo'd no rowm te wok raight, an' wot wi' smoke an' dust frum 't'uther shots beyin' fired, yo couldna sey ote eether'. Yo'd ten yard o'coal te chuck ont pans afore yuh'd got te loosa, an' yo'd te timber up an' aw' afore yuh could goo up t'pit.

The shift over, getting from the coal face to the pit top was a lengthy business:

Wey'd o'must a threy mile traipse te'd pit top frum dairn t'scour wokin's, an' on top o' that, it wor all up 'ill gooin' frum t'uther side o' Strolley Choch! Wey'd pass rippers, an' packers, an' cuttin' machine blokes on us wee aht t'pit. Yo could smell 'em ayf a mile off wi' wind t'wards yuh. . .thi'd smell o' carbolic soap, ale, an' clain moleskins.

At last the men would reach the surface, and fresh air:

It wor grand te gerron pit top, an' com dairn ower t'dot 'ill inter t'pit yard! Yo'd o'must run te t'lamp cabin, chuck lamp in at winder, an' bey off.

Ah canna think on times as good as they wor. Wey 'ad bad times, but te maa reckonin', thi wer none as good. Wey wer a raight good owd set o'blokes!

THE COLLIER'S CHANGING IMAGE

1. c.1877   2. c.1900

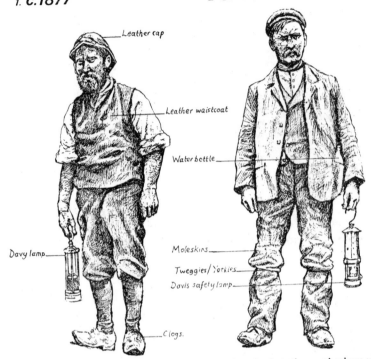

Leather cap

Leather waistcoat

Water bottle

Davy lamp

Moleskins

Tweggies/Yorkies

Davis safety lamp

Clogs

Until the end of the last century, visual records of what the coal-miner wore are extremely scanty — for this area, they are practically non-existent. In the early days, the average collier was, as often as not, simply a worker from the land who dug coal during the off-season. This would have been especially true of Derbyshire, and the Midlands in general, where, until the second half of the nineteenth century, the collieries were small, and the work unspecialized, compared with the larger, deeper pits of the North of England and Scotland.

Protective clothing was rudimentary centuries ago — there is a description by Daniel Defoe of a Derbyshire lead-miner of the 1720's 'cloathed all in leather', with 'a cap of same without brims' — and ordinary slouch hats or soft round caps, flannel shirts and singlets, and breeches, sometimes reinforced with leather, were probably the general wear.

Fig. 1 is a conjectural study of a local face-worker of a century ago. Wooden clogs continued to be worn well into this century; many colliers adding narrow strips of rubber belting to the soles to get a better grip underground. The famous Davy lamp, invented in 1815, continued in use until the late eighteen hundreds.

Fig. 2 wears the typical miner's cap of the period and his heavily-patched moleskins are strapped under the knees to stop dirt and dust from entering. The Davis lamp, made at Derby and Kirkby-in-Ashfield, was used from the last decade of the nineteenth century until around 1950.

Fig. 3 sports the cloth cap and muffler, worn almost universally by working-class men of the between-war period, which are nowadays looked

46

THE COLLIER'S CHANGING IMAGE

3. c.1930
4. c.1977

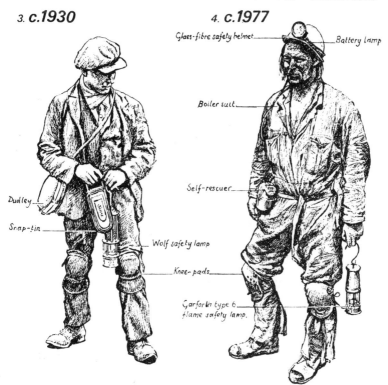

Glass-fibre safety helmet

Battery lamp

Boiler suit

Self-rescuer

Dudley

Snap-tin

Wolf safety lamp

Knee-pads

Garforth type 6 flame safety lamp.

on as an essential part of the miner's traditional image. (Have another look at the 'Ey Up Mi Duck' cover man!). This collier carries a typical 'acme' snap-tin for his packed lunch and a tin 'dudley' which held about a quart of water. The Wolf Safety lamp originated in Germany during the 1890's. The type illustrated is the 1905 improved pattern manufactured in Leeds and in use until the time of the Second World War.

During the late 1930's, shirts of flannel began to give way to cheaper, drill shirts. Different working conditions, even in the same pit, affected what was actually worn on the coal face. In the scour workings at Cossall, which went deep into Nottinghamshire, for instance, it was so hot that miners worked practically naked. A pair of shorts and a pair of boots sufficed. The wetter the conditions, the more clothing was worn, including, from the 1940's onwards, wellington boots.

Fig. 4 is a deputy (based on a photograph of an Ilson man now working at Moorgreen Colliery in Nottinghamshire). Safety helmets, in small numbers, had first been introduced locally during the late 1930's by the Bestwood Colliery Company, and originally they were made of compressed cardboard. Their use became compulsory following nationalisation. Lightweight fibre-glass helmets in various styles first came in during the late 1960's. The type of lamp carried here indicates this man's status. In the early days, deputies carried a stick, and; like other officials, tended to wear their caps back-to-front. Even in later times, they would sometimes wear their helmets in a like manner, or even have them specially made with the peak at the back!

47

QUIZ ANSWERS

1. Is it his?
2. It isn't ours!
3. What's up with you?
4. Have you had a wash?
5. You'll cop it!
6. It's turning to rain!
7. Hark at it!
8. Who was he with?
9. Was he alone?
10. Have you got her with you?
11. How about me?
12. A week on Thursday.
13. Have any of you hurt yourselves?
14. You're not having any sweets!
15. They're good ones, aren't they?
16. Give me half of it!
17. How are you keeping?
18. Are you going to call and have a jar?
19. Have you got it right?
20. I cannot make anything of it!

ON WAGES, WIVES, PRIORITIES AND SUCH

The following poem is one of a delightful series, called 'The Saga of George and Fred', which reflects the life of the coal-mining community in this area during the 1920's.

'Wot duster think o't wages, Fred? Ar don't know air they wok it!
It wouldna bey ser bad, tha knows, it's air't pee office dock it!
My best suit's stoppin' weer it is, I arna gooin' ter 'ock it,
Ber yer wannt yer ale an' Woodbines 'n a bob left i' yer pocket.
An' wen yer'n swallered dust eight hours, yo need a chew o' bacca-
A'll gee air tew bob less this wick; By giney, that'll shack 'er!
Wey storrin' up th' dust aw dee, wile they sit gerrin fatter,
An' wen it coms ter slake us thost, Fred, aw win gorr is watter!
Nair an way ont it, duster think? Wey an, wi'airt a dairt!
Wey need us bits o' pleasure, Fred, eow'll just ay ter goo wi'airt-
Wey stuck dairn't pit threy dees a wick, it ommerst breaks yer back,
Wen ar com up at leowsaw, Fred, ar think ar've done mi wack.
Wen they'n blackleaded rairnd a bit, 'n ponched a few cloos airt,
Thi'n got neowt else ter deow aw dee, thi'n done wi'airt a dairt!
Thi gossip rairnd at neighbours, an' it's yatter, yatter, yatter,
Aah! thi'n got neowt else ter deow aw dee, but stand arairnd an'
        natter.'

'Wot's thi missis deowin' nair, George; is 'er pickin' airt a winner?'

'Neow, eow's mendin' aw mi wokin' cloos, then eow's gooin' ter
    sey ter't dinner.

Eow sits theer wi' a pair o' glasses afe wee dairn 'er nose,

(Thi number eights from Woolworths-thi a 'elp though, ar suppose)'

'Aah! Thi tay'n no notice wot yer sen, shut yer trap, yo might as well,
    son.'

'Ar'm thinkin' soo anaw, owd lad; aw raight, ar'm off ter't "Nelson"!'

ANNE BROWN

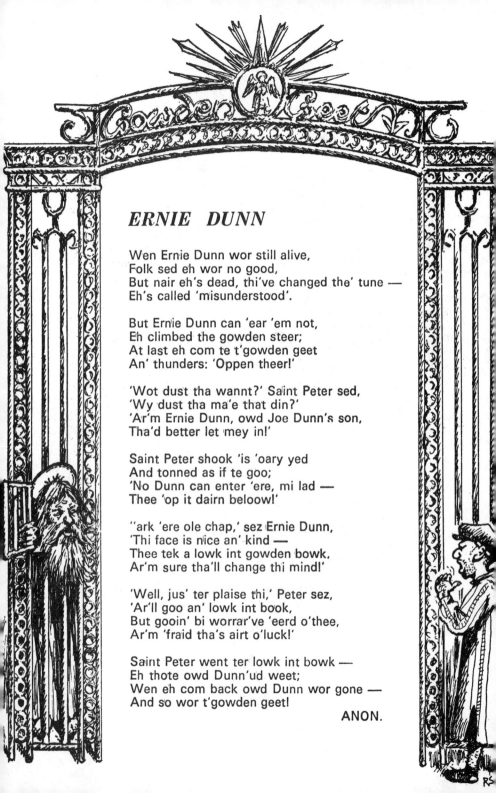

ERNIE DUNN

Wen Ernie Dunn wor still alive,
Folk sed eh wor no good,
But nair eh's dead, thi've changed the' tune —
Eh's called 'misunderstood'.

But Ernie Dunn can 'ear 'em not,
Eh climbed the gowden steer;
At last eh com te t'gowden geet
An' thunders: 'Oppen theer!'

'Wot dust tha wannt?' Saint Peter sed,
'Wy dust tha ma'e that din?'
'Ar'm Ernie Dunn, owd Joe Dunn's son,
Tha'd better let mey in!'

Saint Peter shook 'is 'oary yed
And tonned as if te goo;
'No Dunn can enter 'ere, mi lad —
Thee 'op it dairn beloow!'

"ark 'ere ole chap,' sez Ernie Dunn,
'Thi face is nice an' kind —
Thee tek a lowk int gowden bowk,
Ar'm sure tha'll change thi mind!'

'Well, jus' ter plaise thi,' Peter sez,
'Ar'll goo an' lowk int book,
But gooin' bi worrar've 'eerd o'thee,
Ar'm 'fraid tha's airt o'luck!'

Saint Peter went ter lowk int bowk —
Eh thote owd Dunn'ud weet;
Wen eh com back owd Dunn wor gone —
And so wor t'gowden geet!

                                    ANON.

LOCAL PLACE NAMES—
The Erewash Valley Area
'DB' refers to entries in the Domesday Book, 1086.

Awsworth DB: 'Eldesvorde'. An alternative nine-teenth-century spelling was: 'Ausworth'. Means 'Eald's homestead'.

Borrowash (Traditional pronunciation: 'Burrow-ash'). Other spellings include: Burgo; Burghas; Burysasch; Borowe Ashe. Means 'The fortification or mill near the ash tree'.

Codnor (Pronounced: 'Codna') DB: 'Cotenoure'. Other spellings: Coddenoura; Codden-houere. Means 'Cod(d)a's Ridge'.

Cossall (Traditional pronunciation: 'Cossa') DB: 'Coteshale'. Means 'Cott's corner or cave'.

Cotmanhay (Commonly pronounced: 'Cotmunay'. Traditional Pronunciation: 'Cotmunee'). Nickname: *'Paraffin City'.* Means 'Enc-losure of a cottager', from Anglo-Saxon: 'Cot-mann(ge)haeg'.

Dale Abbey The Dale Abbey area used to be called 'Depedala' (e.g. in a reference of 1158), 'Dale' meaning a valley. It is also referred to as 'de Parco Stanley', from its situation within Stanley Park. Dale Abbey has been designated a Conservation Area; besides the ruins of the Abbey itself, there is the mediaeval church/farm, which is almost certainly unique in Britain.

Eastwood (Traditionally pronounced: 'Eyswood', though natives of the town may well say: 'Eas'wood') Means 'The Thwaite (Scan-dinavian word for an outlying farmstead) situated in the East'. Has no connection with the modern word 'wood'.

Hallam Fields Two hundred years ago, what is now Hallam Fields was known as Bindage Meadow, and was just one of several large meadows which ran down each side of Little Hallam along the Erewash and Nutbrook.

Heanor (Pronounced: 'Heena'; commonly called: 'Eena'; traditionally pronounced: 'Eyna'). It would seem that Victorian newspapers

51

often took a dim view of local pronunciation, as is evidenced by the following entry in the 'Pioneer': 'There is Heanor (not 'Hayner', as it is too often erroneously called)'. D. H. Lawrence, in 'The Rainbow' (1915), spells the name 'Hainor', and says of its houses that they were 'a dry, brittle, terrible corruption spreading over the face of the land. . .' Heanor's nickname, *Tag Tahn* (or *Tag 'ill*) derives from the proper name of an actual part of the town. DB: 'Hainoure'. Means 'The high ridge'. Within Heanor Park lies a deep pond known as *Sookie's 'ole/'oller'*. Dark rumours are abroad of an attempt to rechristen the said 'ole: 'The Italian Gardens'. Yes, well.

Horsley Woodhouse

(Traditionally known as: 'Ossley/Orsley Woodus'). Means 'Houses in the wood belonging to Horsley'.

Ilkeston

(Pronounced: 'Ilkisstun'; the traditional pronunciation, of course, is 'Ilson', which is almost certainly a convenient shortening of the word, as the editors of the 'Pioneer' were once at great pains to point out to one of their correspondents: 'We can only give an hypothetical solution of our correspondent 'Paul Pry's' query: Perhaps it is to economise time or tongue — we use the word 'tongue' in the masculine sense only — or both, that they pronounce Ilkeston with two syllables in lieu of three, which is the legitimate mode: or, perhaps it is to display their wit,—BREVITY being, as everyone knows, or ought to know, the very soul of wit.') Ilkeston was once known as *'Tuppy Land'*. The town appears in the Domesday Book as 'Tilchestune'. Perhaps the most likely explanation for this strange rendering is that it was a mistake made by some cloth-eared Norman scribe, who misheard a local referring to a road leading 't'Elchestun'. The original name of the town was probably 'Elchestun', meaning either 'The enclosure of the Elk' (The Elk—originally 'elch' or 'elcha'—being the name or symbol of an Anglian leader) or, possibly,

'Ealac's dun'—the hill of an Anglian chief called 'Ealac'. Ilkeston has been known by a variety of names since the eleventh century: Elkesdon, Illesden, Ilston, Helkesdone, Helchesdun, Elchesdon, Elcasdona, Hilkesdon, Ilkesdon, Ilkisdon, Ylkesdon, Ylkystun, Ylkeston, Illesdon, Hilson, Ilkestone, Ilkinston.

Kimberley

(Commonly pronounced: 'Kimbly') Means 'Cynemaer's glade, clearing'.

Kirk Hallam

(Commonly pronounced: 'Kok/Kairk Allum'). DB: 'Burhhalum'. Other spellings: Chirchehalum; Kyrkhalm. Means 'Church at the nooks of land'. 'Kirk' is Scandinavian for 'church', and thus indicates a Danish presence in a previously Anglian settlement. Trueman's history maintains that before the church was built, the village was merely part of 'Hallam' ('Hall Ham')—that is, the ham, or village, whose lord lived in a hall. 'Hallam' is also a common local surname and a frequent component in local place-names: Little Hallam; West Hallam; Hallam Fields. On the southern outskirts of the Kirk Hallam estate, near the new Social Club, is what maps refer to as 'Fish Pond', but locals call *'Blood's Pond'*, after the nearby Blood's Farm. Out of deference to our readers, we will refrain from listing gory details, but suffice it to say that the pond has long been associated with various murders and suicides. . .

Langley Mill

Means 'The mill at the long clearing'. Nickname: *'Packie's Puzzle'*. A 'Packie' was the old name for a tally-man (they often carried a *package* or parcel) who would go round houses collecting money from customers who had bought things 'on tick'. Getting his shilling a week out of some people might not be so easy—especially in the area mentioned, where the 'Packie' could well get lost in the 'puzzle' of houses and streets. (A less likely explanation for this unusual nickname is that the 'packie' refers to mediaeval 'packhorses').

Larklands

(Pronounced: 'Larkiuns') The name can certainly be traced back as far as the eighteenth century, at which time 'The Larklands' were situated at the bottom of the Mill Field.

Little Hallam

Two hundred years ago, 'Little Hallam Town', as it was then called, was quite separate from Ilkeston proper. Indeed, until well into the present century people referred to: 'Little Hallam, near Ilkeston'. This area of the town contains a small lane known as *'The Spinney'*, and nearby is Ilkeston's oldest house, Little Hallam Hall. Parts of the building, once the home of the Flamsteed family, date back to the sixteenth century at least.

Long Eaton

DB: 'Aitune' Probably means 'Farm in marshy ground or between streams'.

Loscoe

(Commonly pronounced: 'Losca') Various spellings include: Loftskou (1281); Loscowe; Loskhowe; Loscoo. Means 'Wood with a loft (house)'.

Mapperley

(Commonly pronounced: 'Mapply') DB: 'Maperlie'. Perhaps means 'Maple clearing'. Mapperley itself contains an unadopted road nicknamed *'Cow Muck Row'*, and a bank and field near the reservoir, known as *'Daffodilly'*.

Marlpool

(Traditionally pronounced: 'Marpowl'). The village is only about a hundred years old; previously it formed part of Langley (the 'long field/clearing'). The name derives from the fact that until fairly recently there was a large pond and marl quarry situated on the approaches to Heanor, near the present Marlpool Church. Locals would refer to the pond as the Eighth Wonder of the World, since it was thought unusual to have such a large stretch of water near the top of a hill. The area around Marlpool abounds in nicknames: the long, narrow field between the old Marlpool Station and Newcastle Wood, for instance, is known as *'Pit Pony Dell'*, so-called because pit ponies were commonly kept there during longer miners' strikes—as they were in 1923 and 1926, for example. Adjacent to this is another field nicknamed *'Crack-a-marble'*. The wooded area running down from the side of the Coppice Restaurant to the Cricket Ground is known as *'Dog kennels'*, and the footpath and stream which run between the new housing estate and Mundy Hall on the west side of the main Ilkeston-Heanor road are referred to jointly as *'Askey Sic'*. The name 'sic' appears frequently around this area, and is an Old English word meaning 'a small brook'. Lastly, to return briefly to another canine nickname, the old Marlpool pond site used by the Heanor Urban District Council as a dumping-ground for ashes was known as the *'Dog-nob'*.

Morley
DB: 'Morleia'. Also: Morlege; Morleage; Morlegh; Morleygh. Means 'Moor clearing'. An area near the church is still known as *'Donkey's 'oller'*.

Ockbrook
DB: 'Ochebroc'. Means 'Near Occa's brook'.

Ripley
DB: 'Ripelei'. Also: Ryplea; Rippley; Rippelle. Possibly means 'Clearing in the shape of a strip', but could be derived from the old English tribal name, 'Hrype'.

Risley
Means 'Brushwood clearing'.

Sandiacre
Varieties include: Sandeacre; Saint Diacre. Means 'Sandy piece of cultivated ground'.

Shipley
DB: 'Scipelei' Also, later, 'Sheepley'. Means 'Clearing for sheep'. Shipley was once famed for its good shooting and for Shipley Pike, a tasty dish which used fish caught in traps in the lake. Edward VII, among others, was enticed to visit the hall and grounds, and D. H. Lawrence, in 'Lady Chatterley's Lover', pictures him, still then Prince of Wales, having a conversation with the Squire about coal-mining: '. . .the Prince had replied, in his rather guttural English: 'You're quite right. If there were coal under Sandringham, I would open a mine on the lawns, and think it first-rate landscape gardening. Oh, I am quite willing to exchange roe-deer

for colliers, at the price. Your men are good men too, I hear.' Lawrence can hardly let this pass without an ironical little comment of his own: 'But then, the Prince had perhaps an exaggerated idea of the beauty of money, and the blessings of industrialism.' Like Marlpool, Shipley could once boast of having a 'sic', or small brook, known simply as *'The Sic'*; it flowed from the top of Shipley Common Lane End, under Norman Street, and into the Erewash.

Smalley

DB: 'Smalei'. Means 'Narrow clearing'.

Spondon

DB: 'Spondune'. Also, later, both spelt and pronounced: 'Spoondon'. Means 'Hill where shingle for tiling was obtained'.

Stanley

DB: 'Stanlei'. Means 'Stony clearing'. Stanley's nickname, *'Monkey Park'*, derives from the fact that most of the houses built there during the latter part of the nineteenth century had a 'monkey' or mortgage on them. Within the village certain areas have had their own nicknames: for example, a group of houses, now demolished, used to be called *'Crawcombe'*; then there was *'Klondyke'*, a name given to the houses built at the far end of Morley Lane by the Derby Kilburn Colliery Company. One possible explanation for such a term is that the houses were constructed at the time of the North American Gold Rush. Running due south from Derby Road and the old quarry to Locko ('Locka') Park is a footpath known as the *'Balk'*, which takes its name from a geological fault. Two other local names of the past which owed their origins to mining were *'Sough Lane'*, situated near an old colliery fan shaft, and *'Bore 'oles'*, which bear witness to the old mine workings along the Kilburn Seam.

Stanley Common

Stanley Common was once called 'Smalley Common', and includes *'Nan's Nick'*, a local term for Blunt Street.

Stanton-by-Dale

Means 'Farm on stony ground'. The Risley end of the village is known as *'Barbados'*. Still officially in Stanton-by-Dale, where the outskirts of Kirk Hallam meet Stanton Iron Works, is a row of houses on Sowbrook Lane with the postal address 1-12 New Stanton; to locals they are never anything other than *'Twelve 'aases (houses)'*.

Stapleford Means 'Ford marked by a post'. Nickname: *'Stabbo'*.

Trowell (Commonly pronounced: 'Traal') DB: 'Trowalle'. Means 'Tree stream'. Nickname: *'Tormentalfield'*. Within Trowell lies *'Pig Tod Lane'*, a rather expressive name often given to Cossall Road. The path leading from the 'Festival Inn', past the sewage farm and towards Stanton, is known as *'Trowell Boards'*. It used to be boarded over in places, to act as a pedestrian boardway when the Erewash flooded; it is now tarmaced over. Just to the south of Trowell, on Bramcote Hills, is the famous Hemlock Stone. The name is a corruption of 'Cromleck', from the Welsh 'crom' ('bent') and 'llech' ('flatstone'), and refers to an ancient megalithic tomb.

West Hallam (See notes on Kirk Hallam). Two interesting place-names from this area are *"allam 'oller'*, a traditional and more evocative term for what is now St. Wilfred's Road, and *'Blue Fly'*, the footpath from West Hallam to Mapperley. The path winds between pit soil banks on which Clifton Blue butterflies may sometimes be seen.

Local river names of interest include:

Derwent ('Abounding in oaks'). A Celtic name; one traditional alternative pronunciation is: 'Darent'.

Erewash (Previously 'Irrewysa' or 'Irwis'; perhaps means 'Wandering stream'). Pronounced 'Errywosh'.

Nutbrook ('Brook by which nut-trees grow').

OWD FRED AN' YUNG 'ARRY

Yung Arry: Ey up, Grandad! Ah've fahnd these owd photus int loft . . . This's yer elder bruther, int it, teken durin t'Fairst Wairld War?

Owd Fred: Aar, it is an all! This'd bey wen eh fost joined up. D'yo know, lad, eh joined t'Shairwood Foristers in 1914, an went raight thro th'ole war wi' airt a scratch!

Yung Arry: Worappened then?

Owd Fred: Well, eh wer demobbed, an eh adna bin ut om moore'n tow wick, wen eh got run ova be a tram in Nottingum . . . wey've alluz bin a bit contrary in aar fam'ly! Tek yer gret-uncle Jim! . . . thee brote im airt o't'pit one dee, after t'rowf 'ud fell on is back, an carted im om, thinkin eh wer dead. Thi 'd no sowner gorrim t'ris airse, wen eh oppened is eyes, an sed: 'By Guyney, ar could dow weea pint!' Eh lived fer anuther thoty year! . . awkud bogger!

Bus Stop Scene 3

Lairy begger!

A fellow boarded a train at Ilkeston and found himself in a compartment with three other men. As the train pulled out of the station, he began to fumble in his pockets. Then, turning to the first passenger he said:

    'An yo gorra match?'
    'Neow.'

He turned to the next man:

    'An yo gorra match?'
    'Neow.'

He turned to the third man:

    'An yo gorra match?'
    'Neow.'

In despair he cried:

    'Antonyonyuhonyonyuh?'

SAM TAYLOR

Th'Ilson Giant

SAM TAYLOR

Th'Ilson Giant

This ere's the story o' Sam Taylor. Wey've ad sum big lads rahnd ere, but none on 'em uz big uz Sam! Eh wer born in 1816 in Little 'Allum, wich, fer them uz dunna know, is the bit o' tahn bitwain Kok 'Allum an Ilson proper. Anyroad, Sam wer six foot ten wen ee wer still owny fowertain! Wen ee wer fully-grown, eh wer seven foot fower!

It saims uz aah eh ad a job gerrin a job on accaant on im beyin such a lanky yothe. But then, one dee, wile ee wer mormin arahnd Cassle Donin'ton weer eh'd gone te loke fer wok, eh seyn a tent a'vertisin a 'giant', soo eh peed is penny, an went in t'ay a squint. Apparently, this fairgrahnd vairsion wer owny abaht six foot threy! 'Cause showman tuke one gleg ut aar Sam, an got shut ot't'uther theer'n then. Sam wer signed up direc'ly! (Be all accaants, little giant wer a bit put aht by this tairn o'r'events, an showed aar ee felt by geein Sam a thump. Yung Sam worn't a lad te ta'e this sort o' thing lyin dahn tho', 'an eh sown shut t'uther up by dishin aht a feeow thumps is-sen).

Later, aar 'ero joined up wee anuther travellin show, 'an eventually, eh married t'proprietor's dohter uz did a bit o' glass-blowin fer t'th'entertainment o't'craads. Eh spent most o't' rest o'ris life travellin rahnd wee is missis — 'er blowin glass, an im showin aah tall ee wor.

Sam deyed in Manchester Infairm'ry in 1875, follerin a fall uz'd brok is thigh. Eh might ay gone all ower'd place wee is show, burreh knoo weer te com te be buried! Is body wer brote om be train, an is funeral procession wer accompanied by t'th' Ilson Brass Band! Worra lad!

RS

GLOSSARY

This glossary falls broadly into two sections: a list of words and expressions, arranged alphabetically and a series of other entries, grouped under classified headings. We have mixed words and phrases, and include some non standard pronunciations as well as unusual dialect features.

We have also included more modern dialect expressions along with those which are now quite rare; we have tried not to look upon the older ones with exaggerated sentimentality, though we do believe it is worth a special effort to record, and perhaps even to preserve, some of the more traditional and fast-disappearing dialect phrases.

Any glossary of this type must be incomplete; many readers may well know other examples than those we have included, or may even doubt whether some entries are in common use today.

Abide	To endure, bear. 'Ah canner *abide* 'em.' (I can't stand them). Old English-'abiden'.
Addle	To earn. So in Owen Watson's poem 'The Dignity of Man': '. . .just some o' the things wi purrup we/T'*addle* us daily bread.' (From Old Norse, 'öthla', a variation of 'othal', meaning 'property'. Old English: 'eadlian'.)
A-fire	On fire: also 'A-pairpose' (On purpose).
Afore	Before. (Old English 'on-foran' meaning 'before').
Ah canna git/ Ah can't get	I won't be able to make it, get there. Can also mean 'I'm stuck'.
Ah'd gorrallon	I'd got all on. I was hard pressed, under pressure. As in '*Ah'd gorrallon* te stop mesen laffin'.
Ah dosst jump int cut!	I dare jump in the canal. From 'Durst', the traditional form of the verb 'to dare'. In the negative: 'Ah *dossn't*' or 'Ah *dossna*'. ('I durst not').
Ah'll bost yuh!	I'll beat you up!
Ah'll wam in all dee	I'll stay at home all day.

Ahtdatious	Audacious.
Alarum/Alerum Clock	Alarm clock.
All rahnd Cotmunee te get t'Ilson	Used to describe somebody who is being long-winded: 'Eh went *all rahnd Cotmunee te get t'Ilson'*. (He took a long time to make his point). Also: 'Eh's gone te Bulwell te get t'Ilson'. A similar expression used in Chesterfield is: 'Eh went rahnd Matlock te get te Sheffield'.
A'm—a this aah	I'm of this opinion.
Ah wer all of a shek!	I was all of a shake; I was trembling all over.
A'm bostin'	I can't wait (usually to go to the toilet) or 'I'm in great need of' — as in: *'A'm bostin'* fer a fagl'
A'm gooin te ton me bike rahnd	I'm just going to the lavatory.
Ammer/Ommer	To hit; or a quantity of force: 'Gi'e it sum *'ammerl'*
Anall	As well: 'Ah will, *anall!'*
'Aopen	Perhaps. *'Appen* ee not cum'.
Are yuh arkin?	Are you listening?
Ark ut mey!	Listen to me! (Tradition has it that a local female celebrity uttered this phrase after belching rather loudly at a Civic Dinner many years ago. With a precedent like that, it may be taken as an apology).
As black as Dick's 'at band	Very black in colour.
'Ave yuh done?	Have you finished yet? (Compare 'The Taming of the Shrew' by Shakespeare— Act III; ii; **118** — 'Ha' done!' meaning 'Ceasel').
Awk abaht	To carry about, lug around. Also: 'Ah went 'awkin dahn t'gardin' (I went rushing down the garden).
Ax/Ex	To ask, as in 'Goo 'n *ax* im' or 'Dunner *ex* meyl' (This is not a mispronunciation of the Standard English 'ask', but stems from the Old English verb, 'acsian'). Wycliffe's Bible uses the word as a natural Standard English term: 'Whanne He schal axe — what schal 'y answere to Hym. . .'

Badly	Poorly, slightly ill.
Bartled-up	Bottled up, clogged, or choked; as in: 'Canal's all *bartled-up* wi' weeds' or 'Ah dunna like beyin *bartled-up* rairnd t'neck-ole!' (A Staffordshire variation is 'bartered up').
Battin'	Moving fast, as in: 'Eh wer *battin'* along!' This can also be expressed as: 'Eh'd gorra *bat* on!'
Blather-Yeded	Used to describe a silly person, one whose head is full of nonsense. The same type of person can also be described as 'Bomyed', or a 'Daft/Soft Ayputh', 'Prairtle', 'Ravel-yed', 'Twollup', 'Wap' ('Dunna bey se wappy!') or 'Wesock', etc.
Bletherin/Blitherin	Empty talk, moaning, whining, complaining. Hence the description '*Blitherin* idiot'. (From the Middle English, 'Blather', from Old Norse, 'Blathra', meaning 'nonsense'.)
Blobbed	Stuck out, as in: 'Shey *blobbed* 'er tongue aht ut mey!'
Blortin'	Shouting out. (See also section on Farming).
To bodge up	To make or repair something, making the best of available materials. 'Bodging' can therefore mean simply 'making'. A Staffordshire variation is 'codge'. (Standard English varies slightly from the dialect form — 'To botch up', or 'a botched-up job' means one which is badly or inexpertly done, originally by a 'botcher', a kind of low-grade tailor) Compare 'mank'.
Bogger	Local version of 'bugger'. It carries no dubious sexual connotations, but is rather a mild and even affectionate term of abuse, as in: 'Yuh silly *bogger!*' (The word could possibly have a respectable origin — from the Middle English 'bugge', meaning an imaginary monster). Also heard from time to time is the expression: 'Bogger-up', which can refer to a person who is causing a nuisance, so: 'Yo wait till yuh cum back, *bogger-ups!*'

Bogger this!	'I've had enough!' As in the phrase: '*Bogger this* fer a game o' sowjers!'
Bost-'ead	A damaged skull — as in: 'Eh'd gorra *bost-'ead*'.
Bothered	Keen, as in: 'Oh's not essa *bothered*'.
Brillyunt	Brilliant. Similarly, 'Million' becomes 'Millyun'.
Britches/Breeks	Trousers. From Old English 'bréc', meaning 'clothing for the loins and thighs'.
By guyney!	By Jove! (Possibly a corruption of 'By Guy!' referring to Guy, Earl of Warwick).
A cadey	A boater, or straw hat.
Causey	Pavement. From the Middle English, 'Cauce', which came from the Old French, 'Caucié', 'Chaucié'. (More rarely, the adjective 'Causen' is heard in some areas).
Charlie's dead!	A phrase used when the underskirt is showing beneath the hem of a lady's dress. Sometimes: 'Ah see *Charlie's dead!*'
Chelp	To cheek, answer back; as in: 'Yo've tow much *chelp*, yo ay!'
Chew	To reprimand someone, to nag them; as in: 'Oh wer *chewin* at im all mornin!'
Chuff	To pontificate; hence someone who's sounding off would be told: 'Let's ay less o' yer *chuff*', or 'less o' yer rattle'. There was an old saying, 'Tha's got moore rattle than an empty coal cart', and it may be that 'chuff' comes from the sound the old steam engines used to make when trying to get 'wheel grip' with a full load.
Chunter	To complain, mumble; as in: 'Wot yuh *chunterin* on abairt?' or: 'Yo've tow much chelp 'n' *chunter!*' (see 'Chelp').
Claats	Clothes, and particularly underclothes; compare the expression: 'Ne'er cast a *clout* till May is out'. Ultimately derived from Old English: 'clut', the word for a piece of cloth.
Clack	Noisy chatter. Onomatopoeic From Middle English: 'Clacke'.

Clonk	To hit. Onomatopoeic. 'It *clonked* me ont th'ead'.
Coal Higgler	A man who sold coal, and might 'haggle' over the price.
Cockle-ower/ova	To tip up, over-balance.
Conspicious	Conspicuous.
Cotter	Talk, conversation.
Crampin'	Having a bit of slap and tickle with a young lady. Quite a modern dialect term.
Croodlin'	Crouching down.
Crowed-up	Lucky. As in: 'Eh's a *crowed-up* bogger if iver thee was one!'
Cut	Canal. Ilkeston people refer to the 'Top-*Cut*' (Nottingham Canal) and the Bottom-*Cut*' (Erewash Canal).
Dab in!	Hurry up! Also once used to mean 'cheerio!'.
Dead	Very. As in: 'It wer *dead* good!'
A dead-oss	Refers to doing a job and not being paid for it; can also mean money stopped from a wage-packet.
Derbyshire Neck	A common name for the disease known as bronchocele or goitre. This was once a very prevalent affliction in Derbyshire, as a result of an iodine deficiency in the soil, the county being so far from the sea.
Direc'ly	An old expression meaning 'immediately', 'without more ado', as in: 'A'm commin *direc'ly!'* or: 'Ah s'll be back *direc'ly'*.
Dob im one on!	Hit him! Land him a blow!
Doofer	A 'whatsitsname', or a 'thingamebob'.
Dunna gerrum gooin'!	Don't upset them, set them off again!
Dunna ma'e gam on 'im!	Don't make fun of him! ('Gam' meaning 'game', literally).
Dunna wittie!	Don't worry. If the person being addressed persists in showing every sign of worry, this may change to the slightly less patient form: 'Aw, shut yer wittlin'!'
Dust sey?	Do you see? (Dost thou see?)
Eh belongs (te) them cottages	He owns those cottages—i.e., those cottages belong to him.

Eh'd a-like te com a cropper	He nearly got himself in trouble.
Eh fell ova is-sen	He was eager; as in: *'Eh fell ova is-sen t'elp us'*, or: *'Eh fell ova is-sen* te gerra better view' (or: 'a berrer veeow').
Eh knows all t'wrinkles o't'job	He knows all the details, the ins and outs of the job.
Eh's allus callin' aar Fred	He's always criticizing/gossiping maliciously about our Fred. (The use of 'calling' in this sense is very common in Ilkeston). The word is probably a shortened version of the expression: 'He's always calling Fred all the names he can think of'.
Eh's a snotty-nosed little bogger!	Often directed at scruffy, anti-social children.
Eh's a tidy bogger!	'He's a right one!' Implies that the person referred to is either dishonest or inefficient.
Eh's dressed up like a 'am boon	'He's dressed up like a ham bone'. A comment on a person's attempt to cut a dashing figure. Implies a gaudy and cheap-looking taste in clothes. Similarly the person could be dressed up 'like a thoty-bob piss-pot', or 'a thoty-bob race-'oss'.
Eh's gorra munk on	He's in a very bad mood. Also: 'Eh's gorris wool off'; 'Eh's gorra pig on'; 'Eh's gorra strop on'; 'Eh's gorra cob on'.
Eh worrits te much	He worries too much. ('Worrit?', of course, can also mean: 'Was it?').
Entertain	Tolerate; as in: 'Ah wunner *entertain* plastic flowers int th'aase!'
Epcep	Except.
Essa	Ever so.
Fair	Extremely, very much, really, as in: 'Ah wer *fair* chuffed', or 'It *fair* meks yuh shudder!'
Fast	Stuck; as in: 'Eh's gorris foot *fast* int' railin's.' Can also mean 'constipated'.
Flairt	To throw or flick something. Onomatopoeic in origin.
Flit	To move house. Also used in the pits, for the action of moving the coal-cutting machine. (Middle English 'flitten', from Old Norse 'flytja').

Footpad	Traditional version of 'footpath'.
Forced	Used in expressions like 'Yo not *forced* te like it.' (Standard English, 'You don't have to like it.') or: 'Thee *forced* te catch yuh if y'an't gorra TV licence!' (They're bound to catch you. . .)
Fortnit	A fortnight.
Frit	Frightened.
Frozz	Frozen; as in: 'Ah'm *frozz* te t'marrer!' (I'm frozen to the marrow).
Fun	Found; as in: 'Ah *fun* that photo up int loft'.
Fussy	Pleased: 'Eh's essa *fussy* wee 'is noo car'.
Gab	To talk idly; idle talk: 'Oh's allus *gabbin*'.' (Onomatopoeic in origin, a variant on 'gabble').
Ganzie	Pullover. (Perhaps a garment made from Guernsey wool — compare 'Jersey').
Gellin'	Chasing after girls, (alternatively: 'wen-chin').
Gerraht!	Get out! Meaning: 'You don't say! Well, I never did!' Often said sarcastically.
Get shut	Get rid of. (Standard English slang is 'Get shot of.') as in: 'Ah'd *get shut* on 'em if ah wer yo!'
Gi'e it a waler/ Waler it up!	Wind it up! Give it a go; give it a spin. Often heard when an engine or piece of machinery 'wunna goo'. Also, something which is spinning or rotating can be described as '*walerin* rahnd'.
Gleg	A look; as in: 'Let's ay a *gleg* at it!' The Oxford English Dictionary lists the word as an adjective in use in Scotland and the North, and gives its meaning as: 'sharp-sighted', (from the Old Norse, 'gleggr', meaning 'clear-sighted'). Oddly enough, it was once used in certain parts of Derbyshire to describe a person with a slight squint.
Gnat's cod	A small measurement—a minute distance.
Gone-aht!	Surprised, as in: 'Eh lowked *gone-aht* ut mey!'
Grandad's kicked 'is clogs	Grandfather has just died.

Gulluke!	Go away!
Gu thi wees on	Go your own way.
Guz	'Goes', in the sense of 'says'. Ilkeston speakers will often recount a conversation, not by using indirect speech, but by quoting the exact words spoken, broken up by expressions like 'ah guz' and 'eh guz': "Teacher sent fo' me this mornin', an' ee guz: 'I hear you've been playing truant', an' ah guz: 'Worn't me, sair, musta bin aar 'arry, ee looks jus' like me!'"
Int 'em	A Derbyshire equivalent of the French 'N'est-ce pas?' and German 'Nicht wahr', meaning 'Aren't they?', 'Doesn't she?', 'Isn't it?', etc.
Is it woth ote?	Is it worth anything?
Is that it?	Really? Is that right?
Ite-th	Height. Simply the traditional form of the word.
It fair guz thro yuh!	It's upsetting in some way. It makes one shudder.
It's a corshun!	You'd never believe it! Also: 'Eh's *a corshun!*' (He's a bit of a lad, a bit of a rum-un, needs watching). See D. H. Lawrence, 'The Rainbow': 'Oh, he's a caution that lad — but not bad, you know'.
It's muck'r nettles	It's six of one, half a dozen of the other—the alternatives are the same—it makes no difference.
It's note te dow wi' mey!	It's nothing to do with me!
It wer a raight mush/ mosh	It was a real mess. Also: 'A'm just *moshin* abaht' (I'm just pottering around).
Jiggered	Tired, exhausted.
Jonnock	Fair, just right, genuine; usually used in the negative: 'It's not *jonnock!*' (Variation of 'Jannock': from Norwegian dialect 'Jamn', meaning 'even'. Old Norse 'Jafn').
Kaip that mungrel dairn!	Control your dog!
Keen	Stinging, smarting, as in: 'It caught me ont th' arm, an' it cum *keen* an' all'.
Lad	Used for 'boy'—quite common in the Midlands and North. Also: 'My *lad*' (My son).

Lathered	Dead-beat, tired; literally, lathered in sweat. (from Old English: 'Léathor').
Lawp	To spread something in thick layers, regardless of cost. (In South Derbyshire this becomes: 'Lawpse').
Lend	'Lend' means 'borrow', and vice-versa. So: *'Borrer* mey yer co-at'. (Lend), but: 'Yo cun *lend* mi cap.' (Borrow). Compare the reversal of 'Learn' and 'Teach'.
Lerry	A lorry. (The word 'lorry' itself, in fact, originally came from the dialect verbs 'lurry' or 'lorry', meaning 'to pull, tug').
Let dog sey t'rabbit/cat	Make room. (Standard English slang is 'Let the dog see the bone').
Let's be raight/ Bey raight!	Let us look at the situation truthfully, let's have the truth! Don't give me that nonsense!
Like a station 'oss	Often used for emphasis: 'A'm sweatin' *like a station 'oss!'*
Like one-o	Used to emphasize speed; as in: 'Eh wer runnin *like one-o!'*
Litten	Lit.
A lock-up	A lock on the Canal—e.g. at Gallows Inn, or Awsworth Road.
Lon	*Lon* ('Learn') is used instead of 'Teach': 'Will yuh *lon* me aah te dow it?' This reversal probably stems from the fact that there were two very similar verbs in Old English: 'Laeran' — To teach; and 'Leornian' — To learn. The use of 'learn' in its modern sense is quite recent; Shakespeare uses the word in the sense of both 'learning' and 'teaching'. Compare 'Borrow' and 'Lend'.
Ma'es n'odds/ meks no odds	It makes no difference.
Mam	Mother. What Standard English speakers call 'Mum', or Americans call 'Mom'.
Mank abaht	To muck about, fool around. Sometimes 'to myther and *mank abaht'.* In the Warwickshire/Staffordshire border country, *'mank'* can mean 'cheek'. To *'mank* something up' can also be used when speaking of constructing a thing from old parts, or patching it up. (Compare: 'To bodge up').

70

Mawled	Hot and bothered.
Meggin'	Gossiping, nagging, moaning.
Mend t'fire!	Put some more coal on the fire!
Mester	Mister, or 'the gentleman', as in: *'Mester* next doo-er', or 'Is *Mester* in?' (Is the head of the household at home?) The female alternative, 'Missis', can be used in a similar way.

D. H. Lawrence, in his dialect poem, 'The Collier's Wife', used the word in the sense of 'husband': "E says: Tell your mother as 'er *mester's*/got hurt i'th'pit—'

Mizzled	Disappeared, vanished — as in a conjuring trick.
Mytherin'	To worry or harass; as in: 'Don't *myther* me!' (Don't bother me.) A variation on the rather more familiar dialect words, 'moither', and 'moider'.
Namor	No more: 'Ah've towd yuh, an' ah'll tell yuh *namor*'.
Neyer mind!	Never mind!
No-aah	No-how, out of sorts, as in: 'Ow are yuh?' (ans:) 'Ah fail *no-aah*'.
Nobbut	Nothing but ('note but'), as in: 'Eh's *noburra* yung 'ooligan!' (i.e. only, merely).
Norsed-up	To be thwarted, have one's plans upset, as in: 'Sorry mi duck, if ah *norsed yuh up!*' (I'm sorry if I messed things up for you!)
Ockud/Awkud	Awkward.
Oh, aar!	Yes. Compare: 'Oh, aar?' — meaning: 'Really? Is that so?'
Ollin'	Throwing. As in: 'Eh wer *'ollin'* dot int watter'. (He was throwing muck into the water). The word probably stems from 'hurling', and thus follows a general rule of pronunciation.
Oojamaflip	Used for a 'Whatsitsname'. Also: 'Oojawotsit'.
Th'oss road	The road, as opposed to the pavement (once frequented by horses).
Owd yer sweat!	Take it easy; calm down. Also: ''Owd yer 'osses!'

Own	Recognise; as in: 'Ah wouldn't *own* 'em agen'.
Physic	Medicine.
Piggle	To work away at something with the fingers. A certain spreader of acne.
Plutherin'	Pouring out, billowing; as in: 'This car went past 'n' all smoke wer *plutherin'* aht ot'th'ingin'. (Other dialectal variations are: 'puther', and 'pother').
Poddlin'	Walking; implies a comical gait. Usually describes a small child, or a little old man, etc. As in: 'Eh wer *poddlin'* along wi'aht a care int wold!'
Polled up	Arrived at the scene.
Pol-Thompson	Trouble, 'bovver': 'Ah'll gi'e yuh sum *Pol-Thompson* if yuh not careful!' Probably originates from a local tough character, Paul Thompson.
Praad	Proud, in the sense of protruding or sticking out, as in: 'That length o' wood's a bit *praad* theer, loke'.
Pumps	Gym shoes. Standard English: 'plimsolls'. In parts of South-West England, and in South Wales, the word 'daps' is used.
Pumpture	Puncture.
Raight as a cart	In fine fettle.
A raight 'ockey	A real dump.
Rammel	Worthless rubbish. From the Latin, 'ramale' (a dead bough cut from a tree). An eighteenth century collector of Derbyshire expressions defines it thus: 'Small spraywood left after the cordwood, stakes, and all the larger stuff is taken out. Soapboilers buy it and burn it for ashes. A corruption of French 'ramée', Old French 'ramel'. In the Peak it means 'refuse stone'.' (In North Staffordshire the word refers to a mongrel dog).
Raungin'	Reaching out for something. A variation in Ilkeston is also 'Raumin'', which refers particularly to two varieties of pub competitions. In the one, a person has to touch one beer glass with his thumb and stretch out his hand to push another glass

as far away as possible; in the other he has to hold a penny against the wall, and stretch out as far as he can with his arms without letting the penny drop. The word originates from the Old English, '(a)rae-man', meaning 'to raise, lift up'.

Rawk-up To bring up spittle into the mouth with a rasping noise. (Standard English: 'hawk').

Reckon To adopt. as a policy: 'Thee *reckon* te chuck yuh aht ut closin' time'.

Rezer/Rezevoy/Rezevor Reservoir.

Road Often used where Standard English would use 'way'; as in: 'Gerraht me *road!*' (Get out of my way!) 'Yuh dowin' it wrong *road!*' (You're not doing it in the right way!) Also 'Any *road*/Any *road* up' (Anyway, Anyhow).

Scowul/Skewul School.

Scranny Describes a state where insanity threatens as a result of external pressures. As in: 'If 'im nex-dooer dun't stop 'ammerin', ah'll goo *scranny!*'

Scrat Scratch/Scratched. As in: 'Eh *scrat* is yed 'n' sed. . .' From early Middle English: 'scratte'.

Scrat-up Refers to a shortage of ready cash; as in: 'Ah maniged te gi'e 'em ther bus-fares, burrit wer a *scrat-up*, 'n' no mistake!' (Perhaps a variant on 'a scratch-penny' or mean person).

Scrawk To scratch frantically.

Scrawm To run up, swarm over; to clamber or climb. (Possibly a combination of 'squirm' and 'swarm'). In the children's game, 'snobs', *'scrawmin''* refers to the act of throwing one 'snob' in the air, whilst picking up another off the ground.

Scroddy Puny, meagre, and a bit tatty.

Scrozzle To grope along.

Scruff	Work-clothes. As in: 'Yo niver gooin' aht in yer *scruff*, are yuh?'
Scrummagin'	Pottering around, searching through, as in: 'Wot yo *scrummagin'* arairnd at in them drawers?' (Standard English: 'Rummaging').
Shacken	Shaken or shocked.
Shimmy	To climb or crawl.
Skelp	To hit with the hand: 'Eh *skelped* 'im ont th'ead'. Compare 'to scalp' (Standard English); 'skelfa' (Icelandic: 'to strike'); 'sgealp' (Gaelic: 'a slap'). Middle English: 'skelpen', meaning 'to beat, flog'.
Skinny	Mean; as in: 'Yo've bin a bit *skinny* wi't' chips ant yuh, mam!'
Slorrin'	Sliding.
Sneaped	Snubbed, offended. (From Middle English: 'snaipen', via Old Norse: 'sneypa', meaning 'to nip').
Snyded	Crowded, packed with people; as in: 'It's no good gooin te Macklock tedee, it'll be *snyded* aht wi' folk!' D. H. Lawrence, in 'Sons and Lovers', uses the variation: 'The place is fair *snied* wi' 'em.'
Sorrey-aah!	But of course!
Squint	Like 'Gleg', means 'a look'; as in: 'Let's ay a *squint*, then!'
Starved	Cold; as in: 'Yo loke *starved* standin' aht theer, cum in agen t'fire!' (From Old English: 'steorfan', meaning 'to die, perish').
Ston	Stone.
Strud	Trod/Trodden; as in: 'Loke ut mey, ah've *strud* in sum 'oss-muck!'
Summat's up!	Something is wrong.
Sustificate	A certificate.
Swag	Drink, swig; as in: 'Giz a *swag* o' yer watter, lad!'
Taitered	Exhausted.
Tantazled	Puzzled.
Tantifflin	'Wey in a raight *tantifflin* mess ere!' (We're in dire straights) or 'It's *tantifflin!*' (It's puzzling!). *Tantifflins* are sweet tarts, or sugary delicacies.

Tat-ar	An ordeal, a bad time of it; as in: 'Ah've ad a raight *tat-ar* in them shops this mornin'l'
Taz	A short journey; cruising around in a car, etc. As in: 'Let's ay a quick *taz* rahnd tahn!'
Telewag	Telegraph.
Thar'll knock 'is duck off	That'll take him down a peg or two. The expression originates from the children's game, 'Duckstone', in which a half-brick (the 'duck') is placed on an upturned brick, ready to be knocked off by the other players.
That knocks it inter fits	That beats it hands down.
That's favourite	That's the best plan, the best thing to do.
Thee-etta	Theatre.
Thee not owd im a deal	They haven't got very much control over him.
Thi've got tow chances!	It's up to them! I couldn't care less!
Thronged	Means the same as 'snyded'; as in: 'Cwop wer *thronged* this mornin'.' Note also that 'throng' may be used to mean 'busy': 'As *throng* as Throp's wife.' (From Middle English, 'thrang/throng', meaning 'a crowd').
Time	An approximate time or season of the year. 'It wer August *time*, uz ah remember. . .' Also very common is the expression: 'At that time o'day', which refers to a time in the past, but has nothing to do with a day. So, reminiscing, an Ilkeston man might say: 'Tahn wer different at that time o'day' (at that time).
A time or two	Commonly heard in Ilkeston to mean 'Frequently', 'On several occasions'. As in: 'Eh's fell int' cut *a time or two*'.
Tizzacky	Sick. (From Middle English 'tisik', via Old French 'tisique', meaning 'consumption').
Topside	Above. So, 'Bottomside' (Below).
Tow-rag	An insult: 'Yo note burra *tow-rag!*' (Confusingly, in some areas the word means an 'oat cake').
Trawpse	A long journey, a traipse.

Trutched up	Screwed up tightly: often used if a person puts his arms tightly round his body to keep warm. Often the action of a 'Nesh' person. Some areas use 'Thrutched up', from the Old English 'Thryccan', meaning 'to crowd', 'huddle together'— as in Noah's refusal to let anyone else on his ark: 'We're *thrutched* up wi' elephants!' (Staffordshire: 'Hutched up').
Tucks	Fits of laughter, as in: 'Ah thote me sides wer gunna split, ah wer in such *tucks!*'
Twairtle	To fiddle with something; as in: 'Eh stood theer jus' *twairtlin* wit buttons on is shot'.
Twizzle	To turn around, turn in one's tracks, change direction. Also, to swing something around. As in 'Eh *twizzled* rahnd 'n' ran off'.
Up te press	Up to now, up to the present moment. Or, as Americans and the media insist on saying: 'At this point in time'.
Utch up!	Move a little, budge yourself. As in: '*Utch* yer cheer up a bit!' (Move your chair a little!) or '*Utch* rairnd theer a bit!' (Move round that way a little!).
Waft	To wave, or flick: 'Eh *wafted* a towel ut aar Bert'. (Standard English usage has the sense of some object drifting gently, e.g. a leaf in a light breeze).
Wang	To hurl or throw.
Wazzin'	Urinating: either literally or figuratively: 'Loke at that reen! It's *wazzin'* dahn!'
Well, ah'll goo t'aar aase!	Well I never! You don't say!
Wey raight!	We're all right! Often said sarcastically— i.e. when things are anything but all right.
Wick	There is a well-known ditty which runs: 'Ah'm a Derbyshire man born and bred, Strong i'th'arm and *wick* i'th'ead.' The word *wick* — not to be confused with 'weak' — is a variation on the Old English word 'Cwick', meaning to have life or motion. Compare the Apostles' Creed, 'The quick and the dead'. (The word can also mean 'a week', of course).
Wrong side o't'Brook	Nottinghamshire — the other side of the Erewash.

Yack	To chatter endlessly.
Yawp	To shout. Onomatopoeic. Dates from late Middle English.
Yed	Head. 'Eh wore it on 'is *yed'*.
Yer eye-nee	Sarcastic term describing a person with superior airs. Literally, 'Your Highness'.
Yo wannt bonnin'	You're only fit for burning.
Yuh-begger	Term of abuse often tacked onto the end of a sentence: 'Gerraht on it, *yuh-begger!*'

Black 'n wite meks gree.

Red 'n yeller meks oringe.

Yeller 'n blow meks grain.

Red 'n blow meks pairple.

Red 'n black)
Red, 'n grain)   All ma'e brahn.
Red, blow 'n yeller)

Red, black, wite, blow, yeller 'n grain mek a dotty mess!

DAIRN ONT FARM

Mr Jim Hollingworth and his team of mares, 'Violet', 'Bonny', and 'Trimmer' operating a self-binder — the first to be used in this area — at Bartlewood Farm, Ockbrook, c 1925.

Here we present in words and pictures a very brief glimpse at the local farming scene of yesteryear. Farming, together with mining and offshore fishing, is Britain's oldest industry. Until fairly recent times, agricultural methods had changed little since the Anglo-Saxon era and beyond. It is perhaps not surprising, therefore, to discover that the majority of traditional terms connected with the land are derived from 'Old English' and 'Old Norse'.

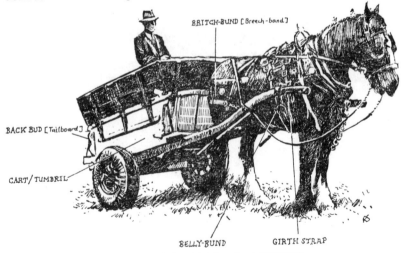

BRITCH-BUND [Breech-band]

BACK BUD [Tailboard]

CART/TUMBRIL

BELLY-BUND   GIRTH STRAP

This drawing of a Farm Cart and Horse in harness, is based on a photograph taken at the West Hallam Ploughing match during the 1920's. Rubber tyres were beginning to replace the traditional cart wheels about this time.

HAYMAKING c1900

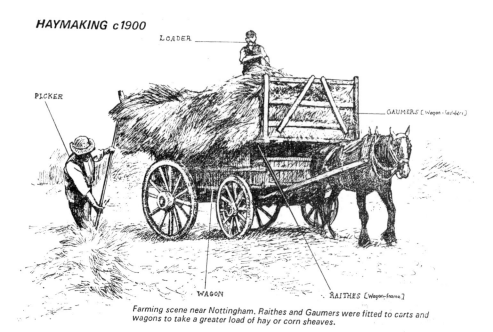

LOADER

PICKER

GAUMERS [Wagon-ladders]

WAGON

RAITHES [Wagon-frame]

Farming scene near Nottingham. Raithes and Gaumers were fitted to carts and wagons to take a greater load of hay or corn sheaves.

RIDGING PLOUGH

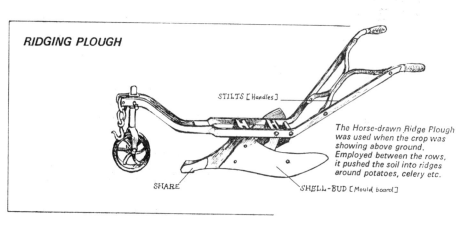

STILTS [Handles]

The Horse-drawn Ridge Plough was used when the crop was showing above ground. Employed between the rows, it pushed the soil into ridges around potatoes, celery etc.

SHARE

SHELL-BUD [Mould board]

HEDGING TOOLS

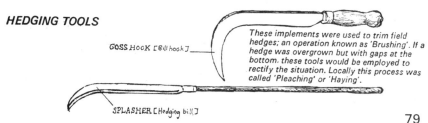

GOSS HOOK [Bill hook]

These implements were used to trim field hedges; an operation known as 'Brushing'. If a hedge was overgrown but with gaps at the bottom, these tools would be employed to rectify the situation. Locally this process was called 'Pleaching' or 'Haying'.

SPLASHER [Hedging bill]

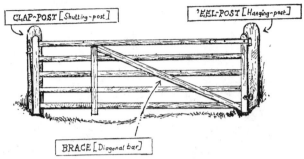

CLAP-POST [Shutting-post]   'EEL-POST [Hanging-post]

BRACE [Diagonal bar]

FARMING GLOSSARY

Adlant Headlands; the strips of land left unploughed at the ends of a field but afterwards ploughed at right angles.

Beestin's The first milk drawn from a cow after it has calved. From Old English 'biesting, bysting'

Cart 'ovel Building which housed farm carts and wagons.

'eel ston (heel stone) Curb at the end of a cow house standing, near the drain.

Muck-cartin' Moving dung from the dung heap to the field.

Seams The ridges of a ploughed field.

Staddle A loosely applied term which can refer either to the base of a haystack or the pieces of timber etc., placed under a stack on the ground to stop the bottom layers getting damp.

Stan'-in (Stand-in) The stall in a cow house where the cows were tethered. The same word described a similar set-up for pit ponies underground.

Taggin' Describes the operation whereby swedes are pulled out of the ground and then 'topped and tailed'.

Thack pegs Used to fasten down a roof of straw covering a haystack. *Thack pegs* were usually of hazel or elder. The word 'thatch' was used to describe a fairly new or dry straw covering. When a stack was threshed, the first job was to take off the thatch, which would now be wet through and also darker in colour than when new. In this condition the word *'thack'* would be used. Hence the old saying: 'As wet as *thack*', meaning: 'as wet as it is possible to get'. (From Old English 'thaccian', 'thac' and 'thack', Icelandic: 'thac').

This n' t'uther The traditional method, in this area, of distinguishing between the near horse and the far horse when both are pulling a wagon side by side.

Tine Hay fork. Sometimes the prong of a fork, from Old English, 'tind', meaning 'the prong or tooth of an implement'. Other traditional meanings include 'the branches of a stag's horn'; 'the prongs of Neptune's trident' or, as a verb, 'to shut a door'.

Wagon A four-wheeled farm vehicle with sides. If the vehicle was without sides, the term 'dray' was used.

Dairn t'Pit.

"TIS COAL THAT MAKES OUR BRITAIN GREAT, UPHOLDS OUR COMMERCE AND OUR STATE.

What follows is a very small selection from the great number of words and phrases we have collected concerned with local mining. The majority of these terms and expressions date back to the days before heavy mechanisation, and have thus fallen out of use. Ilkeston's link with coal-mining today is, of course, rather tenuous, as a result of wholesale pit closures; Ilson pitmen who remain in the town have to travel rather further afield in order to enter 'the bowels of the earth'.

As is the case with many other mining communities, the local pit dialect was affected by the influx of labour from other areas. In the past, local colliers' ranks were swelled by miners from South Wales, Shropshire, Worcestershire, Warwickshire, Staffordshire, South Yorkshire, Northumberland and Durham. (Many of those who moved in from South Yorkshire had, in fact, originated here in Ilkeston). Such an immigration inevitably led to the introduction of new items of vocabulary into the local pit language.

In the 1950's the National Coal Board made a concerted effort to introduce more modern terms of technology into the industry — a move resented and resisted by many men who had spent their lives down the pit; the NCB might refer to an odd-job man as an 'On cost worker', but to lifelong miners, he would always be a 'Daytaler'.

'and-'olin' **(hand-holing)**	The traditional method of coal-getting. Night shift workers, known as "olers', hewed the coal out with a pick.
Bank/Benk	Coal face.
Bantle/Cheer (Chair)	Cage.

Bunkie	Slope or incline where a fault in the coal seam has occurred. A steeper incline was called a 'jig'.
Butty	Originally, a contractor in charge of the entire mine underground; later, a contractor in charge of a team of colliers whose job was to hew out an allotted 'stall' of coal. Nowadays this term simply means 'workmate'. (In other parts of Derbyshire, a workmate is called a 'marrer', a term originating from the North-East of England).
Carfull	A full tub of coal: 'Air many *carfulls* asta fetched tedee?'
Cobbles	Medium sized coal. Selected lumps of trimmed coal were known as 'brites'. Smaller 'cobbles' were called 'nuts', and slack was known as 'peas'.
Collier	Coal face worker. The general term for all mine workers is 'pitmen'.
Dadled	Carried. A miner with an injured leg or foot would sit on the wrist-locked arms of two comrades, his arms around their shoulders.
Daytaler	An odd-job man at the pit. Originally, a man paid by the day, rather than by the piece. '-tale' (which is similar to the modern English word 'tell', meaning to 'count') comes from the Old English. 'talu', meaning 'a reckoning'. The word *Daytaler* dates from at least 1530. To be 'on daytalin'' means to be on day work.
Dooer-Trappin'	The 'dooer-trapper''s job was to open and shut the doors for the tubs to go through.
Dot'ill	Spoil heap or slag tip.
Fast-end	Cul-de-sac.
Fattin'	Greasing the axles of the tubs. This was performed by the 'fat-lads'.
Footrill	Drift mine. First recorded example of the word was in 1686.
Gangin'	Pony driving, performed by 'ganger-lads'. The term probably derives from 'gangan', the Old English verb meaning 'to go'.

Apprentice ganger-lads were known as 'hint-lads'.

Gate	Road. The main road was known as the 'motha geet' ('mother gate'). Other 'gates' included the 'return gate' (airway) and the 'gob gate' (airway filled with dirt).
	('Gate' comes from the Old Norse, 'gata', meaning 'street' e.g. Irongate, in Derby).
Gobbin's	Waste or void area. Hence the phrase: 'Yo wannt *gobbin!*' (You deserve to be thrown away/buried).
Gummins	Dirt or slack from the coal cutter.
Loosall/Loosa	The end of the shift. At this time, colliers who had stripped down for work would 'rag-up', i.e., put their outer clothes back on before making their way towards the pit-bottom. (South Derbyshire — 'Lilly-cock'; Staffordshire — 'Loose-it').
Owd up!	Be careful! Literally: 'Hold your feet up!'
Road	Tunnel or gallery.
Sprag	A small support, usually a block of wood. In everyday speech, a door which keeps springing shut may be '*spragged* oppen' by wedging a small piece of wood or a similar object underneath.
Stall	Length of faee allotted to a contractor; ten yards of coal either side of the (stall) gate was the usual 'stint' for two colliers.
Sweat rag	A piece of cloth or rag worn round the forehead to stop sweat getting in the miner's eyes.
Swilly	Hollow or dip in the road.
Togs/Tugs	Clothes worn down the pit.
Tub	Coal wagon. This term, from the North of England, originally referred to a wicker tub or basket. Other terms for coal wagons include: 'tram', 'busker' (large wagons) 'jotty' (two-sided tub), 'flat jot' (tub without sides).
Tweggies	Straps or fastenings worn around the trouser-bottoms to prevent dust entering.

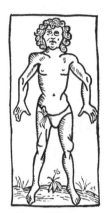

THE HUMAN BODY

Ah'll ay te wesh mi cleck/clock — I'll have to wash my face.

Bonny — Well-built, healthy-looking person—usually describes a baby. (Slightly different from its use in Scotland, for example, where the word means 'beautiful').

Boz-eyed — Cross-eyed.

Clees — Claws, fingers.

Clouty — Dirty. (Compare with 'clarty', common in North-East England and Scotland).

Couldna stop a pig in an entree — A phrase used to describe someone who is very bow-legged; the said pig, of course, would pass between the person's legs and make its escape.

Diddycoy — Used to describe anyone who resembles a gipsy.

Eh's faaler thun a bosted clog — He's very ugly. Alternatives include being 'faaler' (fouler) than 'a box o' frogs', 'a jail dooer', 'ten yard o' coal' or 'a rippin' lip' (The last two examples, of course, having mining associations).

Idle-jacks — Loose skin around the finger-nails.

Lug — A knot in the hair. From the Scandinavian 'lugg', meaning 'a head of hair', and 'lugga', meaning 'to pull the hair'.

Lug 'oles — Ears. (Used as a slang word over quite a large area of Britain).

Oh's faal uz a 'obbin iron — Yet another ugly character.

Oh's like a 'aase (house) side — She's huge.

Ommocks — Feet. As in: 'Shift yer gret *ommocks!*'

Pen-toed	Pigeon-toed.
Potsetten	Filthy. Originally, as 'Pot-sitten', it referred specifically to burnt milk. In the North-East the term 'setten-on' is used for puddings, etc., which are burnt in cooking.
Stickin' aht like chapel 'at-pegs	Protruding; as in: ''is eyes *stick aht like chapel 'at-pegs.*' Also used to describe parts of the anatomy of a well-built young lady.
Tabs/Tab-oles	Ears; as in: 'Did yuh say summat?' 'No, it wer jus me *tabs* flappin!'
Thee reckon uz aah thee yozin yo fer a pipe-clayner	'They say they're using you for a pipe-cleaner.' In other words: 'Aren't you thin!'
Top o't'th'entry	The groin area.

HOUSE AND HOME

Balm	Yeast (Also used for certain herbs). From Old French, 'basme'. Compare Standard English: 'balsam'. The word is used by both Shakespeare and Chaucer.
Cheers	Chairs.
The dogshelf	The floor.
Dolly Peg	Wooden implement used for washing clothes in a tub. Originally fashioned with two arms, and legs and feet, like a doll.
Entree	Narrow passage or tunnel in between houses. (Compare 'Jitty'). Further North, such a passage may be referred to as a 'snicket'. The poet Wordsworth uses the word in its dialect sense: 'It was an entry, narrow as a door'. ('The Excursion', p.71)
Gardin	Garden.
Gennel/Jennel	Steps down between coalhouses into the back-yard.
Illins	Bed linen — sheets and blankets. Once washed during '*Illins*wick' (linen week).
Int winder bottom	On the window sill; notice the stress — 'winder *bottom*'.
Jitty	A small lane. (Dialect words for such a lane or alleyway are legion all over Britain. Examples include: jornal; gennel; opening; woppy-nick).
Pancheon/Panchion	A pan for mixing bread and dough. Originally an earthenware pan for milk. (The 'cheon'/'chion' ending appears to be a diminutive, so the sense is: 'a little pan').

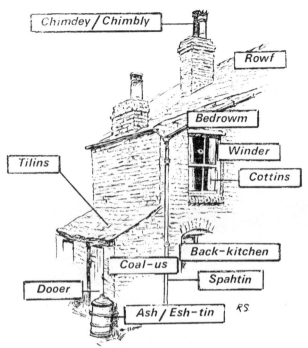

Labels on the illustration:
- Chimdey / Chimbly
- Rowf
- Bedrowm
- Winder
- Tilins
- Cottins
- Back-kitchen
- Coal-us
- Spahtin
- Dooer
- Ash / Esh-tin
- R.S.

Pank-aase (house)	Closet, outside toilet. (Perhaps from 'Plank-House' — since older closets make use of a plank with a hole in it). Other regional words for an outside W.C. include: necessary, nessy, netty, petty, privy.
Ponch tub	A tub used for washing ('punching') clothes — often an old beer barrel would serve this purpose. The stick used in an old copper was also called a 'ponch'.
Pots	The dishes: 'Ah'll goo'n wesh t'*pots!*'
Pumpkin	Pouffe.
Riddle	Coarse sieve, for use in the garden or in building. (The word exists in Standard English, but is more rarely used). From Old English, 'hriddel', meaning 'to shake'.
Squab/Squobenza	Sofa; but a sofa, traditionally, had only one arm — a *squab* had two. The word can sometimes be used to refer to a wash-bench in the kitchen.
Thrall	A stone shelf in a pantry.
Twitchel	An avenue between gardens.
Wesh-us	An outside wash house.

86

THREATS AND COMMANDS

Ah'll cloth yuh one!
I'll hit you!

Ah'll gi' yuh a good tankin'
I'll give you a good hiding.

Ah'll slit yer gizzard if yuh dunna shut yer gob!
If you don't close your mouth, I'll cut your throat! (*'Gizzard'*, from Middle English 'giser', meaning 'the stomach', particularly of birds. *Gob*, probably from the Gaelic and Irish word for a 'beak' or 'mouth').

Bat
To hit; as in: 'Ah'll *bat* yuh one in a minute!' From Middle English, 'battin', meaning 'to hit with a club'.

Be said!
That's enough, that's final; Let's have no more nonsense. 'Ah've towd yuh, yuh norrayin no more chocolate, nah *be said!*'

Clip
To hit; as in: 'Ah'll *clip* yuh one if yuh not careful!'

Gerrup yo, else ah'll bat yer tab!
Get up, or I'll beat you round the ears!

Gi'e ower pipin' yer eye!
Stop crying!

Gob it aht!
Spit it out!

Put wood int th' ole!
Shut the door! (In South Derbyshire, this would often be followed by 'Dusta com fra Oppenwoodgate?').

Scraitin'
Crying. 'Gi'e ower *scraitin!*' (stop crying!) Further North, the word 'scrike' is used for 'shriek'; so 'scraitin', like 'scrike', may have a Scandinavian origin).

Womit!
Go home!

Yo'll ay less!
That's enough from you!

Yo'll cop it!
You'll be in trouble!

THE WEATHER

Ah sey Phoebe's smilin' agen

I see the sun's out again. (From Phoebus, the Greek Sun God, whereas *Phoebe*, or Artemis, or Diana, is really the Goddess of the moon!)

It lokes like it's tonnin te reen

It looks as if it's turning to rain.

It's a ovacoot/ topcoot cowder!

It's cold, it's overcoat weather.

It's gerrin a bit black ower Bill's Motha's

Black rain clouds are building up. Neither Bill nor his mother have ever been satisfactorily identified.

It's 'ollin it dahn

It's pouring with rain. (*'ollin* meaning 'hurling').

It's raight back-end weather

The weather is really autumnal. (First recorded use, 1820).

It's silin' dahn!

It's raining hard. Associated with the act of 'siling', or passing milk through a sieve. Probably of Scandinavian origin, via Middle English.

It's starvin'

It's very cold. (See 'Starved' in general glossary).

It's waarm, int it?

Nice day, isn't it? The important feature of this phrase is the vowel sound in *waarm*, which is an unusual pronunciation for this area.

Mizzle

Very fine rain — finer than drizzle: also used as a verb. Related to Dutch dialect, 'miezelen', and Low German, 'miseln'.

FARMING; ANIMALS AND BIRDS

Back-swathing
Refers to the clearing away of the grass which has been left on the edges of the field by the mowing machine.

Battle-twig
Earwig.

Blackbod
Blackbird.

Blort
To bleat. There is an old Derbyshire proverb: 'A *blorting* cow soonest forgets its calf'. In Staffordshire: 'blart'.

Blowbottle
A bluebottle.

Bod cack
Bird muck. From Middle English, 'cakkin', meaning 'to void excrement'; from Latin, 'cacare'.

Boosing-stake
Tethering-stake.

Buzzer
Bee.

Caa pasty/pat
A lump of dung that a cow leaves in the field.

Cade-lamb
A lamb brought up in the house, because its mother has died. ('Caded' means 'spoilt' and can be applied to humans, especially to children).

Crewe-yard
The yard in which cattle are kept, especially during the winter, for fattening and for producing dung. (Standard term: straw-yard).

Gilt
A young sow. From Old Norse, 'gylt-r'.

Gowdfish
Goldfish.

Hassock
Tussock—a tuft of coarse grass in a field. (See 'Hassock Lane', Shipley.) From Old English, 'hassuc'.

Jennel	The passage inside the cow-house from which the cattle are fed. (See 'gennel'/'jennel' in 'House and Home' section).
Manger	Trough.
Moggi	Mouse; or, sometimes, a cat. In other areas 'moggi' can refer to a calf.
Moldiwarp/ Moudiwarp	A mole. (From Gothic — 'Der Maul' — meaning 'the snout'; Middle English 'Moldwarp/Molwarp'. Modern German is 'Der Maulwurf'). The phrase: 'Eh walks like a *moldiwarp*' may sometimes be heard, meaning 'He walks like a collier'. The connection between a mole and a miner is obvious. One eighteenth century collector of Derbyshire dialect says the word was then pronounced: 'moodywarp'.
Nettle-peggy	Greenfinch. ('Peggy' being a pet-name for 'Margaret').
Oss-muck	Horse manure.
Oss-sting	Horse fly.
Peggy white-throat	Pied wagtail.
Pigsti	Pigsty.
Polled-caa	A cow with no horns.
Runt/Runtling	The smallest, weakest pig of the litter.
Skep	Basket for seeds, used for sowing by hand. (Sowing basket). Also a feed-basket for a horse. From the Old Norse, 'skeppa', meaning 'a basket'.
Spadge	Sparrow.
Spink	A chaffinch. The name imitates the sound made by the bird. From late Middle English.
Starnel	Starling.
Throssle/Throstle/ Trossle/Throbbie/ Thronny	A thrush. From Middle High German, 'Drostel'.
Tup	Ram. From Middle English. In some areas — parts of South Wales, for instance — the word can mean 'mad' or 'crazy'. '*Tup*-'ead' is used for a stubborn person.
Twitch	Couch-grass. From 'quitch', derived from Old English 'cwice'.
Wat-wat	Water-hen.
Wobbie/Wassp	A wasp. Other dialectal variations in other regions include 'wassup' and 'woppit'.
Worum	Worm.

FOOD AND DRINK

Bread 'n bung 'ole   Bread and cheese.

Chitterlins/Chitlins   Pigs' small intestines. From Middle English.

Clammed   Starved, very hungry. As in: 'Ah'm as *clammed* as Baldock's donkey!' Compare 'clemmed'/'clemming', used in many Northern dialects for 'thirsty' as well as 'hungry'. Ultimately derived from Old English, 'clamm', 'clomm', meaning 'cramp'.

Cob   Bread roll. Also used in the phrase: 'Ah wer sweatin' *cobs.*'

Colly nobs/
Nobby Sissons/
Nobby Grains (Greens)   Brussels sprouts.

Dunkin'   Dipping biscuits in a hot drink to make them more palatable.

Frumerty   Barley gruel. Ultimately derived from Latin: 'frumentum', via Old French: 'frumentée' and Middle English: 'frumentee'.
Another local variation is 'flumry', closely related to the Standard English, 'flummery' (from the Welsh, 'Llymru'). Two North Staffordshire words for 'boiled wheat' are worth noting here, namely: 'furmity' and 'frumity'.

Mash   To make tea: tea is always 'mashed' in the Ilkeston area—never 'brewed'. (From Middle English, 'Maschen', meaning 'to

	beat into a mash'. In some areas the word becomes 'mask').
Maziwat	Originally a make of tea, 'Mazawattee'; often used to describe a weak 'cuppa'.
'oles	Ears—referring to pigs' ears, for eating. From 'tab 'oles'.
Omdomuk	Roast potato.
'onkin	A piece of cake or bread.
Passnip	Parsnip.
Patty-cake	Dough left over after baking; sometimes eaten by children. (Compare the rhyme: 'Patta-cake, patta-cake, baker's man. . .')
Scratchin's	Bits of batter left after frying, obtained at a fish and chip shop. (The same thing resulting from frying at home becomes 'scrag ends').
Snap	Originally, the packed lunch carried by miners (in a snap-tin). Nowadays means 'food' in general, as in: 'Ah've ad no *snap* tedee'. (The original mining term possibly originated from the 'D' shaped cans in which miners carried their food; these snapped shut to keep out pit ponies and rats.) In many areas in the North of England, the term 'bait' (deriving from Old Norse, 'beita', meaning 'food') is used.
Sord/Sward	Bacon rind. (From Old English, 'sweard', meaning 'skin; rind of bacon').
Souse	Brawn (pigs' flesh). From Old French, 'sous'. Called 'soused lugs' in some areas.
Squab/Squob	A pigeon ready for the pie.
Stodgin' yer 'odge/ Stuffin' yer 'odge	Eating greedily. (Standard English slang has: 'stuffing your face'.) The Oxford English Dictionary lists the first recorded use of 'stodge' as 1674. Its origin is obscure.
Tonip	Turnip.

THE WORLD OF CHILDREN

Ah bags fog/seg, etc.
I claim first, second, etc. Other regions use 'foggers/foggy/fogs' and 'segger/seggy/seggs'.

Ah'm not frenz o'yo!
I've fallen out with you.

Baalin'/Baawlin
Hitting a wooden hoop along the ground by means of a stick.

Bar-bar!/Bab-bar!
Don't touch!

Bobby
Baby's faeces.

Bobby off
To leave in a hurry.

Bobby's 'at/
Bobby's 'elmet
A roundabout built like an inverted cone, with a rail to stand on.

Bob-o
A horse.

Bowder
A stone or brick ('boulder').

Bum-ball
Parent's term for a ball when talking to very small children. (Onomatopoeic).

Caded
Spoilt. First known use in this sense, 1877. Compare with a 'cade' lamb—one brought up by hand.

To cap (off)
To play truant, skive. Other areas have: 'to play wag' or 'bobbing'.

Case-ball
Football; specifically a leather ball. Sometimes called a 'casey'.

Conk
A lookout; to 'keep conk' (i.e., keeping 'cavey'.) Perhaps from 'conk' meaning 'nose'.

Dick noss
A visiting nurse; so-called because she inspects children's heads for signs of lice.

Div
An idiot. 'You div!'

Dobbin/Stick dobbin
Game involving placing the end of a stick in mud, and then flicking the mud at a chosen target. 'Dobbin' walls was a favourite practice.

Dobs on
A game using marbles — smaller glass ones, known as 'alleys', and larger ones— often made of iron — called 'dobbers'.

93

Other names for marbles were 'taws' (usually made of stone); 'prits' or 'pretties' (multi-coloured glass marbles); 'pops' (from beer-bottles), and 'blood alleys' (glass with red streaks).

Dosser
An old man, tramp. (One who 'dosses down' anywhere).

Duckstone
A game in which a half-brick (the 'duck') is placed on an upturned brick (the 'stone'). One player guards these, while the others throw half-bricks, trying to knock the 'duck' off. Variations include 'Duck on tin', played in the village of Stanley.
The Northamptonshire poet, John Clare (1793-1864) calls it 'Ducking stone':
'I thought them joys eternal when I used to shout and play/on its bank at 'Clink and bandy', 'chock' and 'taw', and 'ducking stone". ('Remembrances').

Eckie
An express train.

Flairtin' arrers
These were sharpened sticks with flights made from old cigarette packets. A piece of string was wrapped round them, and then they were thrown or 'flairted'.

Gadder
A catapult. (Also: 'Gatter')

Glass
Jealous.

Gowdie
A goalkeeper.

Grid/Gridder
A bike.

Guzgogs
Gooseberries (A term used fairly widely in Britain).

Kings/Queens
A truce term in children's games. There are clearly defined regional areas in Britain for different truce terms; other commonly used words, for example in the South and West, are: 'Barley' and 'Fainties'.

Knuckler
A person who plays marbles.

Ligger
Liar. 'Lig' is a lie. (From Old Norse, 'Liuga'). Once common in Standard English.

Muck yer orange
Get dirty/dirty yourself; as in: 'Dunna fall dahn an *muck yer orange!*'

Piece
Wasteground — usually one for playing football.

Pill
Ball: usually a football.

Pin an' button
A prank, in which a button is attached to a window by means of a safety pin, and is then activated by means of a long piece

of thread, making it tap on the window. The joker will usually play such a prank at night time, at a safe distance, and watch his victim come to the window to see who is there.

Pittle
Urine: to urinate.

Pods
Baby boots.

Rusty bum (finger and thumb)/Rustica bomm
A game which involves jumping onto the backs of a team leaning against a wall. Other regional terms for this game include the expressive: 'Hi, Jimmy Knacker'.

Scrag
To pull somebody about. Originally, in Standard English, meant to hang a person on the gallows, to garotte, or wring a victim's neck.

Scronny
Awful, terrible.

Shed
The adjustable cover on a pram.

Sick road
If a children's roundabout is stopped after several revolutions and then sent around the opposite way, it is going the 'sick road'.

Snobs
A game using cube-shaped stones. Elsewhere called 'fivestones', or, if metal-spoked objects are used, 'jacks'.

Spineman
A weedy, feeble person.

Stick
'Versus'; as in: 'It's us lot *stick* rest'.

Stick 'n' geezer
Game involving hitting a piece of wood, sharpened at both ends, with a bat.

Stockin' leggers
Improvised football made up of a bundle of old stockings.

Sucker
Ice-lolly.

Tanks
Toilets, 'bogs'.

Tap
To smack.

Teggies
Teeth (invariably only describes children's teeth). The word 'pegs' is used in some areas.

Ticky
A chasing game; elsewhere called 'Tig' or 'Tag', etc.

Tin-a-lin-a-lairgy/ Tin-a-lirky
A kind of hide-and-seek game involving kicking a tin without being caught.

Trolley
Wooden racing cart. Further North these are called 'Bogies'.

Tuffies/Tutoos
Sweets; any kind, not just toffees.

Wairlies/'elicopters
The winged fruit of the sycamore, thrown into the air so that it descends like a helicopter.

Wale
To hit: 'If yuh don't cum 'ere this minute, ah'll *wale* yuh wen wey gerrom!' From

	late Middle English—originally, 'to mark the flesh with wales or weals'.
Wite 'oss	A game which involves 'tethering' a child near a front door, like a helpless horse, then kicking the door hard until an irate householder comes out to punish the innocent victim. Also sometimes called 'Kick-back-donkey-wite-'oss'.
Wog	To take or steal.
Wun	Won, but used in the sense of 'beat': 'Eh *wun* yuh easy!'

EXPRESSIONS OF EXCELLENCE

Belter	A good one. As in: 'It wer a *belter!*'
Brahma	Excellent. Introduced by soldiers who'd served in India; the word comes from Brahma, the Hindu deity. Also: 'Its a *Brahma*-Rahma!'
Cock-bod	An expression of excellence, as in: 'It wer a *cock-bod!*' (It was a really good one!)
Grand uz ote!	As great as anything — i.e. very great — meaning 'fine!'
Pairler	Like 'cock-bod' and 'belter', this word means 'A raight good un!'
Rasper	Another expression of excellence; often describes a good goal in football.
Ream	First class.
Sahnd	Sound: meaning 'fine', 'great', 'really satisfactory', as in: 'Are yuh *sahnd* yoth?' or 'Wot d'yuh reckon te that LP ah lent yuh?'. . .'*Sahnd!*' or 'Are wey *sahnd* fer a drink?' (Are you still serving?) or 'A'm *sahnd* temorrer naight!' (I've got a date!)

HUMAN CHARACTERISTICS

Ayf-soaped   Foolish.

Brahn   Describes a person who's 'got a nerve'. The implication is that he gets what he wants, and is somewhat insensitive to the the feelings of others.

Cross-obblin   Argumentative.

Doolally   Mad, crazy. (Originally, *'Doolally Tat/ Tap'*—from Deolalie, near Bombay, India, where exhausted troops often had to spend months before going to the coast to be shipped home).

Ee's never-sweat   He's lazy.

Eh's that tight, eh owny braithes in!   Describes a mean person. As an alternative, someone may be said to be so tight that 'If yuh cut 'is throat eh wouldna bleed!'

Eh's thick uz a bull's lip   He's not very intelligent.

Eh's threy shaits (sheets) te t'wind   He's crazy, lunatic.

Faffin'   Fussing; worrying; panicky, as in: 'Stop *faffin'*, thi'll bey ere in a bit!' This type of person may be described as a 'faffer'.

Fawce   The term can mean deceitful, cunning, sly —it was used for a 'fox' in many old dialects, but could be related to the word 'false'. It can also be used to describe a sharp or shrewd person: 'My word, she's a *fawce* little thing. . .a sharp-shins.' (D. H. Lawrence: 'The Rainbow').

Fossneck   A know-all. Hence the expression 'Sey, *fossneck!*' Meaning 'That didn't come off did it, clever dick!'

Gawp   Mouth, in the sense of loud-mouthed. As in: 'Oh's gorra gret *gawp*, oh as!' (Not to

Ignorant

be confused with the verb, to 'gawp/ gaup'—to stare vacantly.) From the Middle English, 'galpen', meaning 'to open the mouth widely; to yawn'.

Rude. If a person you know barges past you in the street without a word, you are justified in retorting: 'Yo *ignorant*, yo are!' The sense is that of a person who is ignorant, or untutored, in the matter of good manners.

Keggy-'anded/ Walick-'anded

Strictly speaking, these phrases mean 'left-handed', but each may also be used to describe a clumsy person. Phrases with a similar meaning elsewhere in Britain include: cack-handed, back-handed, coo-handed, kerry-handed, kay podder, kekky-pawed, bricky, kaggy-handed, skeedy-pawed, skeggy, skitty, etc. (D. H. Lawrence, incidentally, uses the term 'wallit' instead of 'walick').

Lairy

Undisciplined, wild; usually used to describe a bad driver.

Malatrot

Someone who doesn't care.

Manny

Bossy; as in: 'Shey's essa *manny* te them little 'uns!' Has the same meaning as Standard English 'mannish'.

Man-tod

Aggressive, bossy woman.

Mard-arse

Used to describe someone who is 'mardy'.

Mardy

Childish, easily upset, cowardly. Possibly from a spoilt or 'marred' child, who might turn out to be a cry-baby. The word is restricted to an area between Leicestershire in the South, and South Lancashire and South Yorkshire in the North. D. H. Lawrence makes use of 'mardin'' as a verb: 'That's what your mother did for you — mardin' you up till you were mardsoft' ('The Daughter-in-law' I.i.p.21).

Morm-pot

Whining, complaining person—similar to 'mard arse'.

Nasty

Bad-tempered, as in: 'Ee is *nasty*, fost thing in a mornin''.

Near

Parsimonious, tight with money: 'Eh wer that *near*.' Earliest recorded example, in this sense, 1616.

Nesh

Used to describe someone who is soft, or feels the cold easily: 'Wot yuh got yer coot on for, it's not cowd tedee, yuh

	nesh bogger!' From the Old English 'hnesce'—meaning 'soft'.
Oh's gorra pan/gob like a parish oven!	She's got a big mouth — plenty to say.
Oh's not gorrall er chairs ut om	She's half crazy. (Some areas use the opposite, saying of a shrewd person that he has 'all his chairs at home').
Rattle	Refers to a talkative person, who chatters constantly. 'Yo've got sum *rattle*, yo ay!'
Ronk	Roguish. Compare Standard English, 'rank'.
Slutherer	A lazy person.
Stret-eyed	Mean. ('*Stret*' literally means 'narrow', as in 'stretside', used in the pit).
Trudge	A hard-working woman; as in: 'Oh's a good *trudge*, yuh know!'

Air-dow!/Aah-dow!/ Aah-do!	How do you do!
Ahta gooin on?	Traditional greeting. The stock reply is something like: 'Alraight, ahtey?'
Air arta?	How art thou?
Duck	Universal expression meaning 'dear', 'love'. Used for both sexes, and for strangers as well as acquaintances and friends: 'Are yuh alraight mi *duck*?' Also 'Ducky-dido' may be used, especially for children. The Scots choose a different fowl for their comparable expression: 'Hen'. (North-Eastern England: 'Hinny'; American: 'Honey'.)
Ey up!	Universal greeting, also used as an exclamation, as in: '*Ey up*, wot's app'nin'?' Also used to attract someone's attention, as in: '*Ey up*, wot did yuh order, brahn else bitter?'

Flower	Affectionate, friendly term, as in: 'Ow are yuh, *flower?'* (Also more recently popularized on TV by the Northern comedian, Charlie Williams).
K'yo!	Thank you!
My owd	My old—an affectionate term: 'Ey up *my owd!'* (Hello, old chap).
Sorrey	The local version of the traditional term, 'sirrah' (common in Shakespeare). Nowadays, a term of familiarity, as in: 'Eh up, *sorrey!* Aah's it gooin?' Towards Nottingham the pronunciation sometimes approximates more to 'Surrey'. A similar American expression is: 'Yesuree!'
	(Some experts believe the word to be derived from 'Sir Rag'—'Rag' meaning 'a menial'). Samuel Pegge, in his eighteenth century book on Derbyshire expressions, makes a distinction between 'surry', which is used to 'all ord'nary boys', and 'sorrah', which suggests anger of some kind.
Weer yuh purrin' yersens nah then?	Where do you get to these days?
Wot's the crack?	What's happening? What's the situation?
Yoth/Yothe/Youth	Familiar term. Has nothing to do with age — a *youth* can be 16 or 96 — although if an older man is addressed in this way, it is usually by someone near his own age. (By contrast, the term used in much of East Anglia to denote familiarity, also applied to young and old alike, is 'old boy'. A father may refer to his one-year-old son as 'my old boy').
	A nineteenth century editor of Derbyshire dialect sayings defined the word 'youth' as: 'a person, in a half-humorous way'. He goes on to say that the word was obsolete by 1890, 'except in the Peak'. If that were really so, it has undergone a dramatic revival, entirely living up to its name!

THE SLOW AND LAZY LIFE

'Ilkeston. . .a town of idleness and lounging'
(D. H. Lawrence: 'Sons and Lovers')

Aldee	Holiday. The dialectal pronunciation is closer to the original Old English word, 'haligdaez', meaning a 'holy day', than is the more recent Standard English version.
A'm ayin one fer t'body	I'm having a day off work.
Button	A rest, a breathing space; as in: 'Ah'm ayin a *button* fer five minutes'.
A dolt	A lazy person. (In Standard English, a dull, stupid person).
Eh's a raight dull 'un	He's really lazy.
Fast-on	Fast asleep.
Feegalairgy	A mysterious illness, like idleitus or scivitus. So: 'Is Bill norrin wok agen tedee?' 'Naah, eh's gorra tuch o' *feegalairgy!*'
Gerrup! Are yuh gunna lay stinkin' in bed all dee?	Get up!—Do you intend staying in bed all day?
Lorpin' abaht	Hanging around, idling.
Lozzin'	Lounging, not working.
Mahngin'	Listless, aimless lounging, as in: 'Ah get fed up *mahngin'* rahnd th'aase all dee'.
Mormin'	Aimlessly wandering about.
Ormin'	Listless hovering, lounging, loafing, as in: 'Wot yo *ormin'* arahnd at?' May also be used for 'clumsy, shambling'.
Ova-lay	To stay in bed too long. As in: 'Sorry te kaip yuh waitin', burrah *ova-laid!*'
Rawmin'	Roaming.

Slormed	Sprawled out, or lying across something. As in: 'Eh wer *slormed* ova is desk, fast aslaip!' Has the sense of 'spread' or 'covered', properly speaking. D. H. Lawrence uses the word in the sense of 'slushy', 'sloppy'—especially of a young lad very taken with a girl.
Sluther	To drag one's feet, to dawdle along. As in: 'Stop *slutherin'* yer fait in them puddles!' In South Derbyshire, the alternative meaning of 'to slip about—as on ice' is quite common.
Tonk	To travel about; aimless wandering. As in: 'Wey *tonked* arairnd top o't'tairn fer a bit, then boggered off 'om'.

THE PUB

Ah could dow weea pint/kip	I could do with a pint of beer, a sleep—and so on.
Ah've bin up all naight wee a badly rabbit	I've been on the beer/had a bad night.
Arrers	Darts. Sometimes the expression 'Ah'm gooin' dartin'' may be heard.
Beer-off	Off-Licence.
Gerrit dahn yuh!	Drink your beer!
Gerrumin!	It's your round!
It's thaa pee, sorrey	It's your turn to pay.
Popped-up	Drunk. Literally, full of ale or 'pop'.
Slotten	Drunk.
Sup yer ale, yoth	Drink up faster.
Wuffle	Guzzle, drink fast. As in: 'Oh cun *wuffle* it dahn er, yuh know!' (She can knock the drink back!)

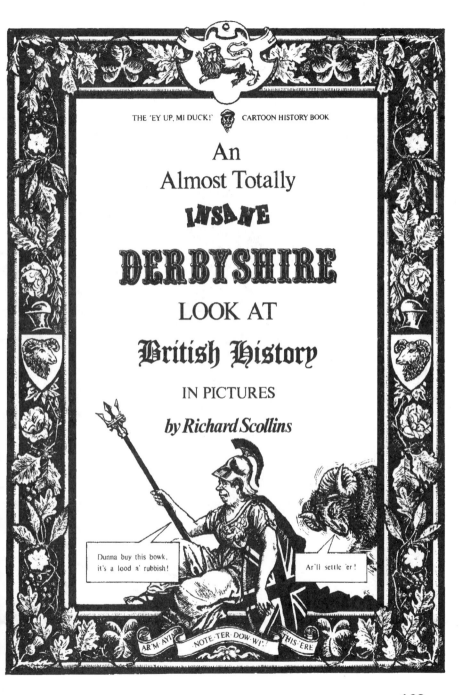

THE 'EY UP, MI DUCK!'   CARTOON HISTORY BOOK

An
Almost Totally
INSANE
DERBYSHIRE
LOOK AT
British History
IN PICTURES
by Richard Scollins

Dunna buy this bowk, it's a lood a' rubbish!

Ar'll settle 'er!

AR'M AVIN.   NOTE-TER-DOW-WI'.   THIS 'ERE

Alfred and the Cakes — AD 878

Canute Demonstrates His Inability to
Turn the Tide — AD 1020

Lady Godiva — AD 1057

The Battle of Hastings — AD 1066

The Death of William Rufus — AD 1100

King John and Magna Carta — 1215

**Edward I Presents His Son as
Prince of Wales — 1284**

Bruce and the Spider — 1306

The Battle of Agincourt — 1415

Richard III at Bosworth — 1485

Henry VIII and Anne Boleyn — 1529

Raleigh and the Puddle — 1581

Francis Drake Goes Bowling — 1588

The First Night of 'Hamlet' — 1601

The Gunpowder Plot — 1605

The Execution of Charles I — 1649

**Charles II and Friends Hide From
the Roundheads — 1651**

Isaac Newton Discovers Gravity — 1666

Bonnie Prince Charlie Arrives in Scotland — 1745

Nelson at Trafalgar — 1805

Wellington Inspects His Troops — 1815

The Charge of the Light Brigade — 1854

Stanley Greets Dr. Livingstone — 1871

Queen Victoria 'Not Amused' — 1878

TH'END.